Heather Davis

LONDON

12 anniversary

Berlitz

D1205918

- A ☞ in the text denotes a highly recommended sight
- A complete A–Z of practical information starts on p.115
- Extensive mapping throughout: on cover flaps and in text

Berlitz Publishing Company, Inc.

Princeton   Mexico City   Dublin   Eschborn   Singapore

Text:	Paul Murphy
Editors:	Tanya Colbourne, Jane Middleton
Photography:	Jon Davison, Jeremy Grayson
Layout:	Media Content Marketing, Inc.
Cartography:	🌀 Falk-Verlag, Munich

Found an error we should know about? Our editor would be happy to hear from you, and a postcard would do. Although we make every effort to ensure the accuracy of all the information in this book, changes do occur.

ISBN 2-8315-6326-7
Revised 1998 – Second Printing May 1998

Printed in Switzerland by Weber SA, Bienne
029/805 RP

CONTENTS

LONDON

LONDON AND THE LONDONERS

London could well be the world's most civilized big city. The roar of the traffic, free of angry horns, is gentler here than in Rome, and the crowds, surging along Oxford Street, and disappearing into the underground, lack the aggression of New Yorkers.

Good manners, you'll soon discover, are a pleasant aspect of British life and this is true in London as well. Step into one of those famous black cabs that glide around town and the driver will discreetly slide shut the glass partition behind him. Ask him for the best place to sample English afternoon tea and he will probably head for the Ritz or Fortnum and Mason, where cucumber sandwiches and scones are served to the accompaniment of soothing classical music. However, if you would like something a little stronger, he can also take you to any number of authentic gleaming gin palaces, some of which even retain their glass snob screens—rather like his own glass partition—designed to keep each to their own.

That much maligned and perennial topic of British conversation, the weather, is actually quite mild in London, and in recent summers has even been almost tropical. On a typical summer's day temperatures rise to the low 20s C (low 70s F) while the thermometer usually stays above freezing in winter. London can be wet, but it is never too gloomy. Those pea-soup fogs of Sherlock Holmes' London are long gone, banished by the clean air legislation of 1956.

By any major metropolitan standard, London is positively pastoral. Contained within some 1,550 square km (600 square miles) are literally hundreds of public gardens and extensive parklands, several of which cover many hundreds

"The way to see London is from the top of a bus — the top of a bus, gentlemen."
William Gladstone

of acres. These verdant open spaces are "London's lungs," and while the city is known for its ecological sins, topographically London is definitely the greenest capital in all Europe.

Through it all winds the River Thames, a blue ribbon of history. Tour boats ply the river in the historical wake of royal barges, between Henry VIII's magnificent riverside residence, Hampton Court Palace, and Greenwich, site of the Meridian. From the boat survey London's glories: the neo-Gothic pinnacles of the Houses of Parliament, the classical dome of St. Paul's Cathedral, and the medieval ramparts of the Tower of London.

If this is your first trip to London, then hop aboard a famous, red double-decker bus. Take the number 11, full of Londoners going about their daily business, oblivious to the sights; or board one of the many special sightseeing tour buses, open-topped for those rare sunny days.

Once you have your bearings, use the underground to get around and trust your feet to do the rest. London repays walkers, with the most interesting architectural details and historical snippets being nearly always found above ground-floor level, where developers and retail façades scorn to interfere.

The city has an astonishing ethnic diversity, much of it a legacy from its old Commonwealth. Indians, Asians, Africans, and Eastern Europeans have all found a home in London. Large Australian and Irish communities have also settled, the former composed of many transitory residents, the latter semi-permanent expatriates in search of London's streets of gold. Perhaps the most visible "newcomers" are the Chinese, who first settled in Limehouse (in the docklands area) a century ago. However, they long since moved to Soho, and have transformed part of it into their own Chinatown.

There is relatively little racial tension in London, and normally streets are safe during the day. At night it is wise to take the same precautions as you would in any large city.

You won't see a fraction of what the city has to offer on your first visit, and you shouldn't even attempt to do so. London is a place to come back to again and again—and, as Samuel Johnson once opined, if you tire of London you really are tired of life.

Horse-drawn carriage in Hyde Park.

A BRIEF HISTORY

The first recorded place name for the city we know today as London was Londinium, established in a.d. 43 by the Roman legions of Claudius.

Julius Caesar had invaded Britain 97 years prior to that, and had crossed the River Thames in the London area. However on this occasion he came, he saw and he left without any trace of a settlement.

Roman London covered just 2.5 square km (one square mile), roughly the area of the modern City, bounded by a

Portions of the Roman Wall—remnants of Claudius's ancient reign—can still be seen in London.

high stone wall. Roman engineers also built the first London Bridge, a basilica, a forum, temples, and many grand villas. Around 50,000 people lived around the two small hills on which St. Paul's Cathedral and the Stock Exchange now stand. You can still see remains of the Roman Wall at various locations, including the Museum of London (where you can pick up a Wall Walk booklet).

From Angles to Normans

The Romans abandoned London early in the 5th century to attend to problems nearer home. Little is known about London during tthe period that followed. The city depopulated and fell into decline, although there is a record of some Britons taking shelter there following the invasion of the Angles and the Saxons in the middle of the century.

At the beginning of the 7th century London received a Christian mission from Rome. The first St. Paul's Cathedral, a small wooden church, was founded and the city began to re-establish itself as a trading port. Then in 851 the Vikings invaded, occupying and destroying much of London. In 886 King Alfred the Great recaptured London and built it up to become the largest city in the kingdom, surpassing even the capital, Winchester. A century later, the Vikings returned and once again occupied the city. They were finally dislodged by King Ethelred II and his Norse ally King Olaf.

1066, the most famous date in English history, is the year the country was last invaded and occupied by a foreign force. William I (or the Conqueror), had a claim to the English crown, and sent Norman armies across the Channel, where he defeated King Harold at the Battle of Hastings. The Conqueror was then crowned in Westminster Abbey (completed only the year before by Edward the Confessor). William subsequently ordered the construction of the Tower of London, not only to protect his new realm from external attack but also to intimidate the people and to prevent a rebellion against the Normans. London, however, negotiated special rights with the new king and prospered.

Feudal England

During the early Middle Ages London's influence grew rapidly while the kings of England were diverted by wars in France and Crusades to the Holy Land. Under King Henry I, its citizens won the right to choose their own magistrates, and during the reign of the absentee king, Richard the Lionheart, the elective office of Lord Mayor of London was created. In 1215, Richard's brother, John, was forced to bow to the defiant noblemen assembled in the meadow of Runnymede (outside Windsor) and set his seal to the Magna Carta. This historic breakthrough in the struggle against tyranny had the incidental effect of confirming the City of London's municipal autonomy.

England's medieval monarchs preferred to keep their distance from the citizens of London. They could be volatile and by now were forming strong trade and craft guilds which still exist today. The Palace of Westminster became the seat of government, and one of the reputed reasons for its chosen site was that its riverside location meant that a mob could never surround the building.

By 1340 London's population was back to around 50,000, but in 1348 disaster struck. The Black Death swept across Eurasia, killing some 75 million people. Details of the horrors in London are scarce, and although there are no accurate figures on the final death toll, it is thought that around one in two Londoners was killed by the disease.

More than 150 years later London still scarcely overflowed the square-mile Roman city limits. The momentous decision by King Henry VIII to break relations with Rome, however, not only gave birth to the Church of England, it also added much needed new property in the form of seized monastery lands. Covent Garden, formerly a Convent Garden, is just one example of church land that was freed for development.

The Elizabethan Era

During the 45-year reign of Henry VIII's daughter, Queen Elizabeth I, England took on the mantle of a world power, and London developed into a great trading port. Elizabeth had wisely built up Britain's navy, and in 1588 it was put to the test when it defeated Spain's "Invincible" Armada. Under the prosperous reign of "Good Queen Bess," the foundations were laid for a colonial empire, and English literature blossomed with the achievements of Francis Bacon, Ben Jonson, and, of course, William Shakespeare.

Steeped in history, the Tower of London was founded by William the Conqueror in 1078.

At that time, however, actors were generally labelled as undesirables and forced to establish their own community outside the City boundary. They did so at Southwark, and in the early 1590s London's first theatreland was established, with the famous Globe opened in 1599.

Revolution and Restoration

In contrast to Elizabeth I's glittering reign, her Stuart successors are remembered principally for their failures. In 1605 James I narrowly escaped assassination in the abortive Gunpowder Plot: Guy Fawkes was discovered in the cellars of the Houses of Parliament about to light the fuse which would have blown up the king at the opening of Parliament on 5 November. On the same date each year, effigies of Guy Fawkes are burned at bonfire parties and firework celebrations.

Statue of Oliver Cromwell (1599-1658) armed with a bible and sword in front of Westminster Palace.

OLIVER
CROMWELL
1599
1658

James I's son, Charles I, was still less popular than his father, and by resisting the wishes of Parliament, he plunged the country into Civil War. In 1642 the Royalists (the "Cavaliers"), supported by the aristocracy, went into battle against the Parliamentary forces. The "Roundheads," named after their short, round hair style, were supported by the tradesmen and the Puritans and led by Oliver Cromwell. The Royalists were finally defeated at Naseby in 1645. Some three and a half years later Charles was found guilty of treason and beheaded in Whitehall.

Cromwell assumed power and abolished the monarchy, and for a short period Britain became a Republic. In 1653 he declared himself Lord Protector and remained so until his death five years later. By 1660 the country had become disenchanted with dreary Puritan rule and the monarchy was restored under Charles II, a great patron of the arts and a famous collector of mistresses (among whom was Nell Gwynne).

Disasters and Recovery

In 1665, a second major plague hit the capital. During that terrible year, 110,000 Londoners perished; the streets were becoming overgrown with weeds and were disturbed only by the death-cart driver's plaintive cry, "Bring out your dead."

No sooner had the city begun to recover from the plague than its festering medieval alleyways, which had encouraged the spread of disease, were swept away in the Great Fire. About 80 percent of the old City area was destroyed, with some 100,000 people made homeless. Incredibly, due to a speedy evacuation there were only eight recorded deaths. Sir Christopher Wren was appointed joint head of a commission to oversee the rebuilding of the new city, and though his grand schemes were never fully realized, he made a massive contribution to the new London, including rebuilding St. Paul's Cathedral and 51 other churches.

Meanwhile new residential neighbourhoods were opening up to the west as developers joined forces with aristocratic landowners to construct the town houses and terraces of the West End. Bloomsbury Square, laid out in the early 1660s, provided a prototype for the elegant squares that were to follow over the next 150 years.

The final great confrontation between king and parliament involved King James II, brother of Charles I. A fervent Catholic, James attacked the Church of England and disregarded the laws of the land. However, the people of England had no desire to cut off another royal head, and in 1688 James was allowed to flee the country. The so-called Gorious Revolution ushered in William of Orange and Mary II to the throne, and established a stable constitutional monarchy at last.

Georgian Growth

During the 18th and early 19th centuries, London became the dynamic and erudite capital of a great world power. In the coffee houses of the City and the West End such brilliant men of letters as Swift, Pope, and Samuel Johnson were holding forth; Handel, the prolific court composer of King George I, was at work on his operas, oratorios, and concertos; Kew Gardens and the British Museum were opened to the public; and Palladian architecture flourished.

But there was a dark side to London. Slums grew up south of the river and in the East End. The urban poor took to drink, adulterated gin being the cheapest tipple, and the crime rate soared. The works of William Hogarth, particularly *Gin Lane*, savagely depict the time when you could get "drunk for one penny, dead drunk for two pennies."

Overseas the Empire was burgeoning, until a tax dispute caused a rift between Britain and the American colonies. This escalated into a full-scale revolutionary war, and to the astonishment of King George III, the colonists won their fight for independence. Even worse, by the end of the 18th century, Britain was threatened with Napoleonic invasion. Admiral Lord Nelson ensured that Britannia would continue to rule the waves by disposing of the French fleet, though losing his own life, during the Battle of Trafalgar in 1805. Ten years later Britain's great military hero, the Duke of

Wellington, put an end to Napoleon's ambitions once and for all at the Battle of Waterloo. By 1801 London had become the world's most populous city, with over a million people.

Victorian Empire

The construction of the docks began in 1802. This assured London's position as the hub of the Empire. As new markets and colonies were conquered, more trade poured through the capital's port.

With the advent of the Industrial Revolution, London was now growing even more rapidly, and by 1861 it numbered some three million inhabitants. Whereas the rich grew richer on the spoils of the Empire, social conditions for the poor were desperate, as documented by Charles

One of London's great military heroes, The Duke of Wellington, is immortalized in Wellington Square.

Dickens. To house the newcomers continually pouring into the city looking for work, the East End slums expanded.

The boundaries of London were pushed well out into the countryside with the development of public transport. Newly invented buses, trains, and, in 1863, the world's first underground railway, created a new breed of London citizen — the commuter.

The indomitable spirit of Winston Churchill looms over London's modern history.

The Twentieth Century

London's first experience of aerial bombardment came from German Zeppelins in 1915, but this was a mere foretaste of what was to come 25 years later. Meanwhile, the inexorable expansion of the metropolis reached its peak in 1939, with 8.6 million people living in the Greater London area.

Hitler's Blitzkrieg rained bombs down on London between September 1940 and May 1941, including one spell of 56 consecutive nights. By the end of the war the death toll was more than 15,000, with 3.5 million homes damaged or destroyed. Through it all strode Winston Churchill, the indomitable spirit of wartime London. You can relive England's finest hour at the fascinating Cabinet War Rooms, the underground headquarters of the British war effort.

Massive post-war reconstruction changed the skyline of London. New skyscraper office blocks now tower unharmoniously alongside Wren's works while the old East End slums have disappeared in favour of faceless high-rise homes, some no better than the ghettoes they replaced. There has been an exodus to the suburbs, and the population of Central London has decreased to what it was in the 1850s.

Today London is still one of the major commercial and financial centres in the world, but its biggest growth industry in recent years has been tourism. Some 16 to 20 million visitors head arrive each year. London may not guarantee sunny weather nor litter-free streets, but its wealth of history is second to none.

London's varied architecture reflects its dynamic history.

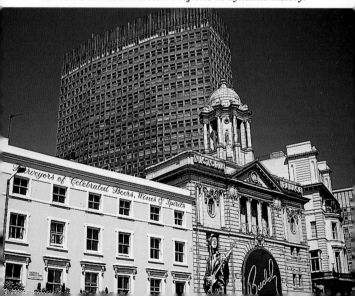

WHERE TO GO

A tour of London usually begins, as it should, with Westminster: the Abbey and the Houses of Parliament, followed by a walk through St. James' Park to Buckingham Palace. From there it's down the Mall to Trafalgar Square, up the Strand to St. Paul's, then on to the Tower of London. Of course, there is rather more to London than these historic sights, but this is certainly a good introductory route for the first-time visitor.

Finding your way isn't difficult in London, and walking or riding on the top deck of a London bus is the most enjoyable, though not necessarily the quickest, method of getting around.

WESTMINSTER AND WHITEHALL

The corridors of power of the British Establishment sprawl throughout Westminster and Whitehall. Symbolic authority centres on Buckingham Palace, the Sovereign's London residence. Nearby Westminster Abbey has been the scene of every coronation since William the Conqueror. Real power, however, is exercised across the street in the Houses of Parliament (or Palace of Westminster), where the government convenes. A short walk away along the street known as Whitehall, thousands of civil servants beaver away behind grey facades, executing the bureaucracy of government.

The Mall and Buckingham Palace

 Start at **Trafalgar Square**, a meeting place for Londoners and tourists from every corner of the globe. The square was named after the naval battle that took place off Cape Trafalgar (southwest Spain) in 1805 in which Admiral Lord Nelson defeated Napoleon. Nelson's statue towers up 52 metres (170 feet) above the square, his shoulders a convenient perch for pigeons.

Grand public buildings like South Africa House, Uganda House, and Canada House face on to the square, but the grandest of all is the porticoed **National Gallery**, housing Britain's greatest collection of European art (see page 70). To the east is the fine Baroque church of **St. Martin-in-the-Fields**, a popular venue for free lunchtime concerts. Its crypt is now a café-restaurant and brass-rubbing centre. On the south side Admiralty Arch frames a splendid view of the **Mall** (it rhymes with "pal"), the sweeping

Admiral Lord Nelson (right) surveys Trafalgar Square, focal point for rallies and demonstrations, New Year's revellers, tourists, and many piegons.

The Queen Victoria Memorial (above) stands outside of Buckingham Palace, the Queen's official residence (below).

boulevard which edges **St. James's Park** (see page 59).

St. James's Palace was the official residence of the court before Buckingham Palace took over the role (1702–1837) and even today all foreign ambassadors are still accredited to "The Court of St. James." The palace itself is closed to the public, however it is well worth exploring the fascinating maze of courtyards and passages, and its Gatehouse is one of London's finest Tudor buildings.

Buckingham Palace, set back behind high iron railings, is to some people a bit dour in appearance, and certainly less romantic than Hampton Court Palace to the west of London. The columned, porticoed façade is the most recent part of the palace, dating from 1913. The palace was originally built in 1702 for the Duke of Buckingham and was remodelled in 1825. The only real splashes of colour are provided by the red tunics of the sentries. When the Queen is in residence the royal standard flag flies overhead.

The palace was opened to the public on a limited schedule for the first time in 1993 and will continue to open during August and September for the foreseeable future. When the main palace is closed you can visit the **Queen's Gallery**, a small modern annexe where exhibitions show works of art from the fabulous royal collection. Further up the street the **Royal Mews** provides opulent stabling for the Queen's horses. The ceremonial carriages they draw are on display in the Coach House, including the fairy-tale Glass Coach which carries royal brides to their weddings and the ornate Gold State Coach which is reserved for coronations.

The Palace of Westminster

The Houses of Parliament occupy the site of the Palace of Westminster. The original palace was built for Edward the

The Changing of the Guard

Everyone should see the country's most popular ceremony once. It takes place daily during the summer and on alternate days during winter (wet weather may cause cancellation).

From 11:15-11:20am the St. James's Palace part of the Old Guard marches down the Mall to meet the Old Guard of Buckingham Palace. There they await the arrival, at 11:30am, of the New Guard, plus band, from Wellington Barracks (on Birdcage Walk, bordering St. James's Park). The actual change involves the ceremonial handing over of the keys of the Palace and the changing of the sentries at Buckingham Palace and St. James's Palace. Meanwhile the band plays informal tunes. When the change is complete (around 12.05pm) the Old Guard marches back to Wellington Barracks and the St. James's detachment of the New Guard marches up the Mall to St. James's Palace.

Confessor, c. 1065, and for 400 years was a royal residence. The only remaining medieval part of the Palace is Westminster Hall (1099). The rest went up in flames in 1834, making way for the monumental neo-Gothic structure you see today. Sir Charles Barry was the driving force behind "this great and beautiful monument to Victorian artifice," completed in 1860. His assistant, Augustus Pugin, provided the inspired Gothic decoration but, literally driven mad by the work, died before its completion.

Magnificent statue of Richard the Lion-Heart in front of the Palace of Westminster.

The public is only admitted to the House of Commons and the House of Lords to hear government debates, although en route to the former you can snatch a glimpse of the splendid medieval interior of Westminster Hall. It was here Sir Thomas More, Guy Fawkes, and Charles I were all tried and condemned to death. To avoid the lengthy wait for these sessions, British residents should apply well in advance to their Member of Parliament and foreign visitors to their embassy in London. Admission times to the House of Commons are Monday through Thursday 4:15 P.M. onwards and Wednesday through Friday 9:30 A.M. onwards, and to the Lords Monday-Wednesday from 2:30 P.M., Thursday 3:00 P.M. onwards, and Friday 11:00 A.M. onwards. On Tuesday and Thursday afternoons you can see Prime Minister's Question Time in the Commons. Both houses recess from August to October, and Christmas and Easter.

From Parliament Square you can see some of the exterior of **Westminster Hall** (to the left of the public entrance to the Commons). But more impressive is the river elevation—a counterpoint of pinnacles and spires, the square bulk of the Victoria Tower balanced by the clock tower of **Big Ben**. This 13½-ton bell marks the hours with a chime known all over the world. The clock's hollow copper minute hand measures 4 metres (14 feet), which makes it about the same height as the double-decker buses passing below the tower. The name is thought to commemorate Sir Benjamin Hall, Chief Commissioner of Works at the time the bell was cast in 1859, but it may also have been named after a popular boxer of the day, one Benjamin Caunt.

Big Ben, London's most famous landmark.

Westminster Abbey

Westminster Abbey is Britain's coronation church, a royal mausoleum, and a national shrine. Kings and queens lie buried here alongside eminent statesmen, soldiers, scientists, musicians, and men of letters. The High Altar has been the scene of every coronation for the last 900 years—as well as many royal weddings. But the Abbey remains a house of worship with services taking place on Sundays, when the highly acclaimed Westminster Boys' School Choir sings.

The nave is open daily, free of charge, but you have to pay to see beyond the screen where the Royal Chapels, Poets' Corner and other areas of interest lie (closed on Sunday). Regular Abbey "Supertours" are conducted by vergers, and if you are keen to see everything amid the crowds this is 90 minutes well spent. Go to the information desk in the nave for details.

The West Door leads directly into the **nave**, which soars to a height of nearly 31 metres (102 feet). The first grave that you will pass is the **Tomb of the Unknown Warrior**. It is a great irony that here among so many great statesmen and members of royalty the most famous and most visited tomb is that of an unknown soldier. His body was brought back from the World War I battlefield of Flanders and represents the 765,399 British servicemen killed in the war. It is the only floor tomb in the nave upon which it is forbidden to tread on,

---

The Mother of Parliaments

England had a parliament long before the country became a parliamentary democracy. As early as the 13th century, representatives of the whole country—nobles and burghers alike—came to consult with the king, either at the Palace or in the Chapter House of Westminster Abbey.

By the mid-16th century, when Parliament moved permanently to the Palace, the body had divided into Commons (spokesmen from the communes, i.e., the provinces) and Lords.

Today there are 650 Members of Parliament, elected to the Commons by universal suffrage. The House of Lords comprises 1,200 members: hereditary peers, life peers, Law Lords, and bishops. Their function is to review and revise bills proposed by the Commons, but they can also initiate legislation, debate national issues and sit in judgement as the highest Appeal Court in the land.

and even royal processions detour around it.

Beyond the screen is **Statesmen's Corner**, where many British Prime Ministers are buried, including Gladstone. The royal tombs lie around the **High Altar**. Moving anti-clockwise you will see the final resting places of Edward I, Henry III, Edward III and Richard II. In the centre of the Altar is the **Coronation Chair**, a great, battered oaken throne used for the crowning of every monarch since 1307.

Further into the church the **Chapel of Henry VII** is breathtaking—ablaze with the banners and pennants of the Order of the Knights of the Bath (an old chivalric order), adorned with intricately carved wood and masonry, the stone fan vaulting above as delicate as lace. Henry commissioned this masterpiece in 1503 to serve as his final resting place.

Westminster Abbey— Coronation church, royal mausoleum, and national shrine

Around the chapel (moving counter-clockwise) are buried: Elizabeth I and ("Bloody") Mary I—sisters, but religious enemies, sharing the same tomb; Henry VII; the Stuart Monarchs —a vault holding Charles II and William III; and Mary Queen of Scots. Walk back past the High Altar to **Poets' Corner** where Chaucer, Spencer, Dickens, Hardy, Kipling, and

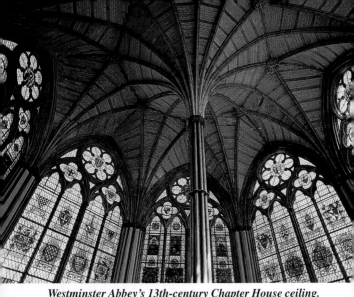

Westminster Abbey's 13th-century Chapter House ceiling.

Browning are buried. You'll find memorials to almost every literary figure you can name, although most of them are actually buried elsewhere.

A side door exit takes you to the **Great Cloister** area, which includes the octagonal **Chapter House**, where Parliament once sat, as well as the ancient **Chapel of the Pyx** and **Abbey Treasures Museum.** A single ticket covers admission to all three. There is also a brass-rubbing centre in the Cloister area.

Seats of Power

Whitehall is the area of government buildings that extends from Parliament Square to Trafalgar Square. The name comes from Henry VIII's Palace of Whitehall, of which the Banqueting House is all that now survives.

Heading along Parliament Street you pass the imposing late-19th-century headquarters of the Treasury. Some 3 metres (10 feet) underground sprawl the once hidden **Cabinet War Rooms**, Churchill's command post during the war years (entrance at Clive Steps in King Charles Street). Within this blast-proof labyrinth the War Cabinet sat over 100 times to prepare and co-ordinate plans. All clocks in the complex are frozen at 16.58 hours, 15 October 1940.

Just a few yards away is **Number 10 Downing Street**, office and residence of the prime minister since 1735. Unfortunately gates have been erected that keep the general public a considerable distance away, so Number 10 can only be glimpsed as the house with the protruding lamp over its porch and police officer outside the front door.

The Tower of London is still guarded by beefeaters.

Old Scotland Yard—of Sherlock Holmes and Hercule Poirot fame—is tucked away between Whitehall and Embankment at 6 Derby Gate. The buildings are now used as government offices. Parliament Street becomes Whitehall at the junction with the Cenotaph, the monolithic memorial commemorating the dead of the two World Wars. A little farther on is the **Banqueting**

Two London "bobbies" at the entrance to 10 Downing Street.

House, built in 1619 by Inigo Jones for James I as England's first truly Renaissance building. Its major feature is a splendid Baroque ceiling by Rubens, commissioned by Charles I.

Horse Guards, on the west side of Whitehall, duly maintain their traditional sentry posts, as this is still the official entry to the royal palaces, even though Whitehall burned down in 1698 and St. James's Palace has long ceased to be the main royal residence.

A guard change ceremony takes place at 11:00 A.M. Monday to Saturday and 10:00 A.M. on Sunday, and an inspection is carried out at 4:00 P.M. Through the gates lies Horse Guards' Parade, scene in June of Beating the Retreat and Trooping the Colour (see Calendar of Events on page 90).

The elegant green-domed building adjacent is the **Old Admiralty**, built 1725. Here Nelson took his orders and eventually lay in state. (The building is open to the public by appointment only.)

Doing the Strand

The Strand links Westminster to the City along a route opened in Edward the Confessor's time. Today it is a busy thoroughfare of shops, commercial premises, and theatres. Take a bus and watch the sights from the window; the world-famous Savoy Hotel, a monument to Art Deco; the imposing Somerset House, home to the **Courtauld Institute Galleries** (see page 73); and the Baroque church of **St. Mary-le-Strand**, stranded mid-Strand in the churning traffic.

Down on the Embankment, parallel to the Strand, the traffic is still heavy, but there are riverside views. Here, too, you will find London's oldest outdoor monument, a 21-metre (68-foot) Egyptian obelisk, called **Cleopatra's Needle**, cut from the quarries of Aswan c. 1475 B.C. (it was one of a pair—the other one stands in Central Park in New York City). It was presented by the Viceroy of Egypt in 1878 as a memorial to Nelson and Abercrombie, who had defeated the French at the Battle of the Nile in 1798.

Away across the river is the **South Bank Arts Centre**. This is the home of the Hayward Gallery, the Museum of the Moving Image, the National Theatre, the Royal Festival Hall, and the National Film Theatre. Although the grey concrete building complex is one of London's least attractive landmarks, the quality of entertainment here is on a par with that anywhere in the world.

THE CITY

The City (short for the City of London) takes care of business. Every working day 300,000 commuters pour into the area colloquially known as "the Square Mile" and busy themselves with banking, insurance, commodity and share trading, and every other kind of financial dealing. At 5:00 or 6:00 P.M. they pour back out again, leaving a comparative ghost town of some 6,000 residents. It is therefore vital to visit the City during office hours when the area is alive and pubs and restaurants are in full swing. Even the churches in the City close on Sunday.

The Square Mile extends east–west from the Tower of London to the Law Courts at the junction of the Strand and Fleet Street and north–south to the Barbican from the Thames. This was the area originally enclosed by the Roman Wall. Despite much new development, there are still narrow lanes and alleyways to remind you what the medieval street pattern must have looked like, and exploring on foot is the only way to see the City.

Legal London

Legal London starts at the very edge of the city with the **Royal Courts of Justice** (better known as the Law Courts) on the Strand. These remarkable buildings (finished 1882), complete with Gothic turrets and pinnacles, resemble more a Bavarian castle than the home of English civil law. A few yards opposite across busy Fleet Street a tiny alleyway leads to the gas-lit sanctuary of the area known as the **Temple**. This houses two of the four **Inns of Court**, Inner Temple and Middle Temple. In former times they were the residences of barristers and barristers-in-training. Even today barristers-in-training must be members of an Inn.

The Temple takes its name from its 12th- and 13th-century function as the home of the crusading Knight's Templar. Visitors have access to the round Temple church, built in 1185. The magnificent 16th-century Middle Temple Hall is open to the public Monday through Friday from 10:00 to 11:30 A.M. and 3:00 to 4:00 P.M. if not in use. Walk up Chancery Lane, past the **Public Record Office Museum** (repository of William the Conqueror's Domesday Book, Guy Fawkes' confession, Wellington's Waterloo despatch, and other compelling bits of reading) to the ancient gatehouse of Lincoln's Inn, above which Oliver Cromwell once studied.

Lincoln's Inn has legal records dating back to 1422, making it the oldest of the four Inns. The Old Hall in front of you dates back to 1490 and the adjacent New Buildings are only new by the Inn's standards, dating back some 300 years. The gardens here are particularly beautiful and are open Monday through Friday from noon to 2:30 P.M. Head back along Chancery Lane to High Holborn, turn right, continue for about a hundred yards, and you'll come to the entrance to **Gray's Inn** next to the "Cittie of Yorke" public house. This is the smallest of the Inns, with no buildings open to the public. The gardens are still worth a visit, however. Sir Francis Bacon was a member here, and his

The Royal Courts of Justice appear more like a Bavarian castle than a courthouse.

statue stands in South Square. Young Charles Dickens was apprenticed to a firm of solicitors at Number 1 South Square in 1827, earning a wage of 13s 6d (67½p) per week. Pop into the historic Cittie of Yorke for a drink after seeing the gardens.

Fleet Street

Make your way back down along Chancery Lane (or Fetter Lane) to Fleet Street, a name that is synonymous with

*Sir Christopher Wren's masterpiece, St. Paul's Cathedral
was begun in 1675 and completed in 1708.
A church has stood on the site since Roman times.*

British journalism. The printing industry was established
here nearly 500 years ago, but in the last decade the major
British newspapers once forming the hub of Fleet Street life
have almost all moved to new premises to the east in London's Docklands.

Plenty of historic associations with men of letters
remain in the area, however. Visit **Dr. Johnson's House** in
Gough Square and see where the first definitive English
dictionary was compiled, then follow in his footsteps by
popping round the corner to enjoy a drink at **Ye Olde Cheshire
Cheese**. Dickens also drank here, and so little has changed that
he and Johnson would probably still feel quite at home.

St. Paul's Cathedral

Christopher Wren was not only the first architect to supervise the construction of an English cathedral single-handed, but he also had the good fortune to live long enough to see his dream realized. He is buried in the crypt of St. Paul's. The Latin epitaph on his plain tomb translates: "Reader, if you seek his monument, look around you."

Balance and clarity here, as elsewhere, distinguish Wren's design. The interior is awesome. Among the most outstanding elements are Grinling Gibbons' beautifully carved choir stalls, Tijou's wrought-iron choir screen and gates, and, of course, **the dome** itself. This is the second largest in the world (after St. Peter's in Rome), rising to 111 metres (365 feet). Climb up to the first level, the **Whispering Gallery**, and ask someone to stand opposite you. Put your ear to the wall and you can hear even a whisper, 33 metres (107 feet) away. A total of 627 steps ascend to the very top for dizzying views of the City.

Westminster Abbey may hold the royal remains, but there are also many famous monuments and tombs in St. Paul's. The most notable are those to the Duke of Wellington and Admiral Lord Nelson. Don't miss the **statue of John Donne** rescued

---

Wren's Prodigious Output

In 1663 Wren was asked to make repairs to Old St. Paul's Cathedral which had stood for over 500 years. He recommended that it should be completely remodelled, but this was rejected. However, the Great Fire of 1666 paved the way for his design. Although his only engineering resources were manpower and pulleys, Parliament was nonetheless exasperated by the slow rate of progress and halved his already meagre salary of £200 to £100 per annum. During this time he was also engaged on 53 churches, The Royal Hospital at Chelsea, The Monument, Hampton Court Palace, St. James' Palace, and the Royal Naval Hospital at Greenwich.

The magnificent dome of St. Paul's Cathedral dominates London's skyline.

from the ruins of Old St. Paul's Cathedral. The great poet was Dean of the cathedral and his likeness, wrapped in a funeral shroud, is scorch-marked—a legacy from the Great Fire.

The Cathedral is open Monday through Saturday 8:30 A.M. to 4:00 P.M. to view the dome galleries and the crypt, and on Sunday for services only.

After visiting the cathedral call in at the City Tourist Information office in St. Paul's Churchyard for literature and advice relating specifically to City attractions and events. Their telephone number is 0171-332 1456.

The Barbican

A windswept concrete jungle, is home to the **Barbican Arts and Conference Centre**. As with the South Bank Complex its architecture has won few friends, but here too the cultural offerings are excellent, and include picture galleries, theatres, a cinema, bars, and restaurants. It is also the London home of the Royal Shakespeare Company and the London Symphony Orchestra. Go along at lunchtime for free foyer concerts.

The other pride of the Barbican Centre (just outside the Arts Centre) is the excellent **Museum of London** (see page 36). For a more general history lesson on the kings and queens of Britain, visit **Royal Britain** (opposite Barbican

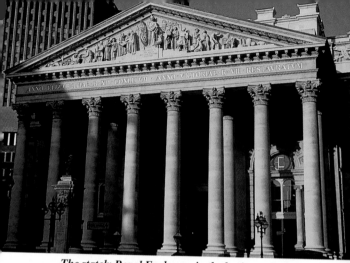

The stately Royal Exchange in the business district.

underground). Various audio-visual effects and tableaux of the past make learning fun.

The Financial City

The heart of the business district of the City focuses, not surprisingly, on the **Bank of England** (nicknamed "The Old Lady of Threadneedle Street"). Imposing windowless walls rise impregnably, with seven storeys above ground and three below. This is where the nation's gold reserves are kept. The bank no longer deals with the general public, but there is a small museum (entrance on Bartholomew Lane).

The tower block next door to the Bank of England is the **Stock Exchange** building and just across the road the splendid classical structure just across the road is the **Royal Exchange**, built 1844. Opposite the Bank of England is another classical-style building, the 18th-century **Mansion House**, official residence of the Lord Mayor of London during his or her year of office (open to group tours only).

The Lord Mayor of London is the First Citizen of the City, though not of the rest of London. The office dates back to 1192, and the most famous incumbent was Sir Richard (Dick) Whittington, elected on four occasions between 1397 and 1419. In 1983 the first female mayor was elected. Among the more interesting privileges is the right to be buried in St. Paul's Cathedral if the incumbent dies in office (as happened in 1885), as well as being granted access to the password of the Tower of London.

Next to Mansion House is possibly the finest of Wren's City churches, **St. Stephen Walbrook**. Its lovely dome is said to have been a rehearsal for the larger cupola of St. Paul's, and the interior was restored from 1978 to 1987.

Due east of the Bank of England, along the ancient thoroughfares of Cornhill and Leadenhall Street, is **Lloyd's of London**. Lloyd's originated in 1688 in Edward Lloyd's Coffee House, where ships' captains, merchants, and ship owners would gather to exchange news and carry out marine insurance deals. Lloyd's moved to the space-age building designed by Richard Rogers in 1986. A huge atrium rises 61 metres (200 feet) at the heart of this steel and glass structure which, like Rogers' Pompidou Centre in Paris, exposes everything to view. Only pre-booked groups are admitted to the building, which contains a fascinating small museum.

In the shadow of Lloyd's, the Victorian cast iron and glass of **Leadenhall Market** is altogether more down to earth. The quality of the fruit, vegetables, and poultry have been enticing City dwellers here since the Middle Ages, and the slightly shabby but friendly atmosphere is always lively and colourful.

Just south of here, **The Monument** raises its flaming urn in memory of the Great Fire of London in 1666 which swept away the medieval City. The Monument towers 61 metres (202 feet) high, the exact distance due east to the site of the baker's shop in Pudding Lane where the fire started.

Northwest of the Bank of England, along Princes Street and Gresham Street, is the **Guildhall**, the town hall of the City. This resilient building dates from

Lloyd's of London, the city's most controversial building.

1411 and has withstood the Great Fire and the Blitz. Step inside (during office hours) for a free look at the ancient Great Hall. Here the functions and ceremonies of the City of London carry on today as they have for centuries: banquets of state, the annual swearing-in of the new mayor in November, and every third Thursday (except in August) the Court of Common Council meets. The banners of the twelve principal City Livery Companies (craft guilds whose members once wore a distinct livery) hang around the Hall. In total there are 94 Livery companies and their members elect the Lord Mayor.

Around the Tower

The **Tower of London** is London's greatest historical sight. Throughout its 900-year history it has been a fortress, a royal palace, and a notorious prison and place of execution.

The Monument memorializes the Great Fire of London that raged through the city in 1666.

Grim though its history is, the Tower looks benign enough today, surrounded by pleasant green lawns. Stormed by over two million visitors a year, the fortifications are manned by 41 Yeomen Warders. Known as "Beefeaters," these ex-military gentlemen dress in Tudor costume and give continuous free introductory tours, which are both informative and most entertaining. If you want to beat the crowds, arrive early. Note that each February the Crown Jewels are closed to the public and there is a reduced entry charge to the Tower.

Your tour will pass by **Traitors' Gate**, which was the river entrance to the Tower before the Thames was moved back. Those unfortunate enough to be deemed traitors were brought here by boat. Above the gate is Edward I's Palace, home to the King in the late 13th century and the only surviving medieval palace in England. The **Bloody Tower** (opposite) takes its name from one of the most dire deeds in British history. The "Little Princes," Edward V and Richard, were interred here in 1483 by their uncle, Richard of Gloucester, and were never to be seen again—though two centuries later two small skeletons were discovered nearby. Another famous occupant was Sir Walter Raleigh, who "lived" here, with his family and servants, from 1603 to 1616.

Tower Green is the site of the execution block, where six noble persons are known to have lost their heads. These include two of Henry VIII's wives, Anne Boleyn and Catherine Howard, and the "nine-day Queen," Lady Jane Grey. Commoners, including Sir Thomas More, were executed in public outside the Tower walls on Tower Hill, in front of crowds of up to 200,000 people.

After visiting the beautiful, though melancholy, chapel of **St. Peter ad Vincula**, where lie the headless bodies of many famous execution victims, head for the **Crown Jewels**. The royal regalia dates largely from the Restoration of Charles II in 1660. The Crown of St. Edward, named after the Confessor, was made for the coronation of Charles II and has been used at every coronation since. It is so heavy at 2 kilograms (5 pounds) that it is exchanged at the first opportunity for the Imperial State Crown. Studded with some 3,250 jewels, this holds the Black Prince's ruby and the Second Star of Africa.

The **Royal Armouries** in the White Tower are thought to be as valuable as the Crown Jewels. Don't miss Henry VIII's huge suit of armour or the Oriental Armoury, which includes an even bigger suit, created for a battle elephant! The **White Tower** itself is the oldest part of the Tower of London, and the **Chapel of St. John** dates from 1080.

Look into the Wakefield Tower, where Henry VI was murdered, and stroll along the **Wall Walk**, where prisoners were allowed to take the air. Look out, too, for the Tower ravens; according to legend, if the ravens ever leave, then both the Tower and England will fall. New ravens are bred and their wings are clipped to ensure that they will stay.

Below the Tower is **Tower Bridge**, one of London's most famous landmarks. This marvel of Victorian engineering, clad in Gothic-style stonework, matches the Tower in appearance. Overhead walkways provide magnificent panoramic views up and down the river. Exhibits illustrating the history of the bridge can be seen at the Tower Bridge Museum.

East of Tower Bridge is **St. Katharine's Dock**. At the peak of its trade in the mid-19th century these warehouses provided storage for up to 100,000 tons of exotic cargos, including ostrich feathers, turtles, and ivory. It was never a great commercial success, however, and has been attractively redeveloped into commercial and residential use, complete with early 20th-century Thames sailing barges. Moored opposite the Tower on the south bank of the river, the **H.M.S. *Belfast*** saw action in World War II and Korea. You can take a ferry from Tower Pier and look over the entire ship to gain an insight into conditions of war at sea.

THE WEST END

Despite its name, the West End is in every sense the centre of town: a focus for theatre, nightlife, shopping, entertainment, smart hotels, and restaurants.

Oxford Street and Piccadilly are the most famous streets and form the approximate north–south boundaries of the West End. This also takes in the central neighbourhoods of Mayfair, Soho, St. James's, and Covent Garden.

Piccadilly

West End sightseeing usually starts at **Piccadilly Circus**, where neon lights have shone brightly for more than a century. The celebrated traffic circle (the meaning of Circus) has been pedestrianized and is a favourite meeting point for tourists and locals alike.

Tower Bridge raises its bascules about three times a week to allow tall ships to pass.

The famous statue of **Eros** caused quite a fuss when it was erected in 1893. Dedicated to a philanthropist, the Earl of Shaftesbury, it was intended to represent the Angel of Christian Charity, and not, as it has become known, Eros, the Greek God of sexual love. The naked statue shocked Victorian morality and was considered totally inappropriate.

The recently redeveloped Piccadilly Circus has all the neon of old plus two new shopping and entertainment complexes aimed at the casual tourist. The **London Pavilion**, once a music hall, now pulsates to **Rock Circus**, Madame Tussaud's venture into rock and pop wax figures (see also page 76).

One of the main attractions at the adjacent Trocadero Centre is the fascinating **Guinness World of Records** exhibition, effectively the show of the popular book. Segaworld

The statue of Eros against the glitz and bright lights of Piccadilly Circus.

occupies seven floors and is the world's largest futuristic indoor theme park. The rest of the Trocadero is young, brash, loud, and very touristy.

Just a few yards away is Leicester Square (pronounced "Lester"), another busy meeting place, where the big West End cinemas feature first-run blockbusters. Here also are nightclubs and the Society of West End Theatre (SWET) half-price ticket booth (see page 87).

Piccadilly (the street) links Piccadilly Circus to Hyde Park Corner. Among the mile-long stretch of airline offices, shops, and hotels, the square brick tower of **St. James's Church**, **Piccadilly** signals a charming oasis. This church is considered one of Wren's best—and it is also now home to a peaceful courtyard café. Across the street is 17th-century Burlington House, home of the **Royal Academy of Arts**, which regularly shows exhibitions of international fame.

Alongside the Royal Academy is **Burlington Arcade**, one of the oldest and most exclusive of the capital's covered shopping promenades, built 1815 to 1819.

Just as exclusive is **Fortnum and Mason**, where shop assistants in tails preside over purchases of caviar and quails' eggs in what must be the grandest grocery department store in the world. For a truly English experience take afternoon tea at Fortnum's. Or, if Fortnum's isn't quite your cup of

Darjeeling, why not try the **Ritz**? Afternoon tea here is another of London's great (if rather pricey) institutions. The Ritz backs on to Green Park, the smallest of the royal parks.

Piccadilly ends at Hyde Park Corner. Facing Wellington Arch (also called Constitution Arch) is **Apsley House**—with the most exclusive address in town: No. 1, London! This was the for-

The London Pavilion is now the home of Rock Circus, a rock-and-roll wax museum.

mer residence of the Dukes of Wellington, and is now home to the **Wellington Museum**. Some fascinating memorabilia, including the swords of Napoleon and Tipoo Sultan, recall the epoch of British history when the Empire was built by force of arms and Wellington was its commander. There is also a very fine collection of paintings by several Old Masters.

Mayfair

That most aristocratic of London addresses, Mayfair, lies to the north of Piccadilly, between Park Lane and Regent Street. All the most elegant shops and exclusive clubs are to be found here. But Mayfair wasn't always so grand. The

---

Victorian Shopping Regulations

Victorian High Society was very concerned that common riff-raff should not be allowed to spoil the dignity of Burlington Arcade, and they laid down strict rules which are still in force today. Uniformed beadles may eject anyone who is running, whistling, singing, or carrying a large parcel or open umbrella!

---

name recalls the boisterous May Fair, held at Shepherd Market during the late 17th and early 18th centuries—a notorious haunt of prostitutes. Indeed, today **Shepherd Market** is hardly a paragon of virtue. By day it is the charming village centre of Mayfair, with Georgian houses, small food shops, antique shops, cafés, restaurants, and pubs. By night, however, it is something of a red-light district, though by and large the night prowlers and residents seem to maintain neighbourly relations.

The most famous Mayfair addresses are the early Georgian squares—Berkeley (pronounced "Barkly"), Grosvenor (pronounced "Growvner") and Hanover (pronounced as you think!). Sadly, little remains of their original properties or charm. You would be fortunate to hear a nightingale sing in Berkeley Square above the traffic noise and Grosvenor Square is now known as "Little America," after the largest, and quite probably the dullest, embassy building in Britain.

Don't go shopping in **Bond Street**, Old or New, without your credit cards. Cashmere, jewellery, Old Master paintings, and fine antiques are the stock in trade here. The presence of **Sotheby's** (34 Bond Street), the world's oldest firm of art auctioneers, says much about the street. Running north from here, Savile Row kits out Britain's—and some of the world's —best-dressed men. Large luxury hotels line Park Lane, no longer a lane now, but a boulevard with bumper-to-bumper traffic, day and night.

Marble Arch, at the top of Park Lane, is the gateway to Oxford Street, but it used to be the gateway to hell, as between 1388 and 1783 this was the capital's place of public execution. In 1571 the notorious Tyburn Tree, a triangular scaffold on which 24 people at one time could be hanged, was erected here. During this period it is estimated that around 50,000 people were executed. (For more gory details see the London Dungeon on page 74.)

The monumental **Marble Arch** was designed by John Nash to celebrate the victories of Trafalgar and Waterloo, and was originally erected in front of Buckingham Palace in 1827. Nash was concurrently working on the design of the Palace, but owing to budget over-runs he was dismissed, and in 1851 his Marble Arch was moved to its present site. By now Nash was so unpopular that his detractors spread the delicious rumour that the arch had been moved because it was too narrow to accommodate the Sovereign's royal coach. This story is quite untrue but is so firmly embedded in London lore that you will even hear tour guides repeat it as gospel!

Designed by John Nash in 1827, Marble Arch originally served as the main entrance to Buckingham Palace.

Baker Street was made famous by Conan Doyle and his character Sherlock Holmes, whose legendary residence at 221b is commemorated by the **Sherlock Holmes Museum** (open every day 9:30 A.M. to 6:00 P.M.).

Run the gauntlet of **Oxford Street** if you're in the mood for serious shopping in the big stores. Be prepared though: it may be a "must see" on the tourist agenda, but the street is nearly always overcrowded, especially on Saturdays and at lunchtime. Regent Street is less hectic. Here you will find **Liberty's**, for fabulous floral fabrics; **Hamley's**, the world's largest toy shop; and **Garrard's**, the Crown Jeweller.

St. James's

Officers and gentlemen frequent St. James's, the area south of Piccadilly. Here in the heart of clubland (gentlemen's clubs, not nightclubs) you will find centuries-old wine merchants, hatters, shirtmakers, and shoemakers who cater for the most discerning masculine tastes.

The famous **clubs**, beloved of Jules Verne's Phileas Fogg, Beau Brummell, and other 18th-century gentlemen, line Pall Mall and St. James' Street. Don't look for signs, though, announcing any names, as discreet anonymity is the watchword. Today, there are fewer than thirty clubs, but St. James's is still a male bastion. Even the art and antique dealers display leather armchairs and sporting pictures straight out of the defunct clubs. **Christie's** auctioneers on King Street has been Sotheby's gentlemanly rival since 1766.

Some of the shops in this area resemble time capsules, usually only seen in museums. You can order a top hat from **Lock's** (established in 1759), handmade shoes from **Lobb's** (established 1849), or vintage wines from **Berry Brothers and Rudd** (established 1699). Have a look in their windows at the very least.

The area derives its name from **St. James's Palace**, which stands between Pall Mall and the Mall (see page 21). At the end of Pall Mall is the **Duke of York's Column**, a memorial to George III's impecunious son, who was the Commander-in-Chief of the British Forces. The Duke died with debts of over £2 million and the statue was paid for by deducting one day's pay from every officer and soldier. This unpopular measure helped condemn his memory; the nursery rhyme about the

"Grand Old Duke of York" who marched his men to the top of the hill and then back down for no apparent reason was a satirical comment on his indecisive nature.

Soho

The popular image of Soho as a seedy red-light district is fast becoming outdated. There are still prostitutes and there are still sex shows, but by international standards Soho is safe for the casual tourist. Nowadays it is better known for its vast choice of international restaurants.

A stoic guardsman helps maintain security at St. James's Palace.

Its cosmopolitan make-up dates back to an influx of Huguenot and Greek refugees in the 17th century. Soho soon became a melting pot for many European nationalities, and most recently a significant Chinese community. Atmospheric Old Compton Street is a good example of the area's multinational flavour, with an Algerian coffee shop, an Italian delicatessen and restaurants representing France, Italy, Malaysia, Vietnam, and the United States. Pâtisserie Valerie on this street is one of London's favourite tea shops.

The **Chinatown** district centres around Gerrard Street. Street names here are subtitled in Chinese, and the tops of telephone boxes resemble mini pagodas. Eating out is the major attraction. Tuck into *dim sum* during the day at one restaurant, and then come back at night to sample wind-dried duck at another. Follow Wardour Street across Shaftesbury Avenue into the heart of Soho and pass the 17th-century ruin of St. Anne's Church, with its strange, barrel-shaped clock tower. At the eastern edge of Soho is **Charing Cross Road**, the centre of London's antiquarian book trade, with many charming, dusty old second-book stores.

☞ Covent Garden

Covent Garden's name is a corruption of "convent garden," a reminder that before the Dissolution of the Monasteries this land was cultivated by the monks of Westminster Abbey.

Developed with patrician town houses in the 17th century, Covent Garden became a bohemian area of pubs and coffee houses, popular with writers and artists. Rather like its neighbour, Soho, it was definitely seedy (home to many brothels) and, at times, downright dangerous. It is no coincidence that London's first police force was established here in Bow Street.

A market for fruit and vegetables was set up in the 17th century and so thrived for over two centuries that the permanent **Central Market Halls** were built in the mid-19th century. However, traffic congestion finally meant the departure of the market to South London in 1974 and the redevelopment of Covent Garden. Since then all kinds of trendy shops, markets,

We are the world — Chinatown comprises one element of Soho's multinational flavour.

Covent Garden bustles with activity seven days a week, drawing crowds with its many shops, markets, and restaurants.

restaurants, bars, and museums have been attracted to the area, most of which stay open late seven days a week. The wine bars and restaurants open late, too, making Covent Garden a popular after-theatre rendezvous.

Inigo Jones' striking **St. Paul's Church** holds down the west side of the Piazza and here London's very best buskers entertain. All are auditioned in advance to make sure they are good enough for the discerning Covent Garden crowd.

The old Flower Market hall to the east accommodates the charming **London Transport Museum** (see page 66) and, the **Theatre Museum** (see page 66) next door is one of London's unsung treasures, reflecting that "the Garden" is at the heart of the performing arts in London. Here, too, you'll find rock music venues (The Rock Garden, where U2 and Dire Straits

Harrods Department Store is proud of its motto "omnia, omnibus, ubique — everything for everyone, everywhere."

once played), theatres, and the world-famous **Royal Opera House**, home of the Royal Opera and Royal Ballet companies. Backstage tours are given at the Theatre Royal in Drury Lane.

Take time out to wander the tiny alleyways, particularly the charming, gas-lit **Goodwin's Court**, which connects St. Martin's Lane to Bedfordbury. The lovely bow-windowed houses date from the late 18th century. Health-conscious foodies should head for **Neal's Yard**, hidden away off Neal Street. A bakery, café, and food shops cluster round a quaint cobbled courtyard.

Bloomsbury

London's most erudite district is heavily associated with the early 20th-century literary life of the Bloomsbury Group, an association of artists and writers including E. M. Forster, Virginia Woolf, and Roger Fry. The neighbourhood is characterized by several charming squares, where blue plaques mark the many homes of the famous. The **British Museum** (see page 61) and the University of London are also in this area.

Almost a century before the Bloomsbury Group made the area famous, Charles Dickens lived and worked at 48

Doughty Street, and his home is now **The Dickens' House Museum**. Take children to see the charming little **Pollock's Toy Museum** (1 Scala Street; see page 75).

LONDON'S VILLAGES

Scores of villages have been woven into the urban fabric of London. Originally each boasted its own high street, church, green, pubs, and local character. Most of these have now been subsumed into the anonymous urban sprawl that makes up much of Greater London, but here we concentrate on five that are on the edge of central London and are well worth exploring.

Knightsbridge

Hardly a village in the traditional sense, but if you are waiting for the bus near Harrods, look across Brompton Road to the triangular shape of **Kensington Green**. This was the village common of the humble hamlet of Brompton 150 years ago. It is now one of London's most desirable residential and shopping areas.

Harrods, with a staff of 5,000, is probably the world's most famous store. Opened by Henry Charles Harrod in 1849 as a small grocer's shop, the present terracotta palace, with its famous façade lit by some 11,000 light bulbs, was built at the turn of the century. The services Harrods can offer are legendary and the store claims to be able to supply any merchandise anywhere; in 1975 the staff proved the point by sending a baby elephant to Ronald Reagan, then Governor of California. The highlight of the store is the extraordinary Edwardian **Food Halls**, exquisitely decorated with 1,902 tiles and featuring an extravagant fresh fish display which changes daily.

Beyond Harrods and its fashionable neighbour, Harvey Nichols, is **Beauchamp Place** (pronounced "Beecham"). The

A Chelsea Pensioner shows off his scarlet coat, worn only for special occasions.

former village high street is now a high fashion street with some very pricey restaurants and designer shops. Brompton Road and **Sloane Street**, the main shopping arteries, converge beyond the green with Knightsbridge, a wide avenue running parallel to Hyde Park.

Kensington

Kensington skirts the red brick palace where the Princess of Wales lived and Princess Margaret continues to have apartments. **Kensington Palace** has been a royal household ever since the asthmatic William of Orange fled the polluted, damp Whitehall. You can tour the historic State Apartments and see the Court Dress Collection. The front lawn of the palace are the lovely **Kensington Gardens** (see page 59). Just a few yards from this peaceful world is the hustle and bustle of **Kensington High Street**. Chain stores dominate the High Street, but behind are elegant white stucco terraces with gardens of tangled greenery. Off here, next to the neo-Gothic church of St. Mary Abbots, is **Kensington Church Street**, famous for its antique shopping.

South Kensington ("South Ken") is famous for its **museums**, a legacy of the Great Exhibition of 1851. The **Victoria and Albert Museum** (known as "the V&A") is the best-known and biggest, but the **Natural History Museum** and the **Science Museum** also offer fine collections (see pages 64-65). Everybody will find something to enjoy here, but don't try to see more than one museum a day (the V&A requires several visits).

Chelsea

Chelsea has been at the cutting edge of London fashion for decades. Mary Quant started it from the first boutique (long-gone) on the **King's Road**, and from the World's End (at the west end of King's Road) avant-garde designer Vivienne Westwood and Malcolm McLaren (manager of the Sex Pistols) gave the world the punk craze in the late seventies. Chelsea in the nineties is rather more subdued, and the King's Road tends nowadays towards chain stores and the odd idiosyncratic boutique, but a walk along it always provides good people watching.

Some of the brightest garments are in fact worn by the area's oldest and most conservative residents, the **Chelsea Pensioners**. Everyday attire is a navy blue uniform, but when attending events as guests of honour they dress in their famous scarlet coats, whose design dates to the 18th century. Their home is the **Royal Hospital**, a landmark in Chelsea since 1692, best approached from Royal Avenue. Charles II founded this retirement home for old and disabled soldiers, and today more than 400 army veterans reside here. The Hospital chapel and Great Hall are open to visitors most mornings and in the afternoons (closed at lunchtime). Between the Hospital and the Embankment, the well-tended lawns of Ranelagh Gardens host the world-famous **Chelsea Flower Show** every Spring. The modern building on the far side of the hospital houses the **National Army Museum** (see page 68).

Continue down to the River Thames along Royal Hospital Road and turn into **Tite Street**. This attractive residential area is the very picture of bourgeois respectability, but a century ago it was a very bohemian neighbourhood. Look out for the blue plaques on Tite Street dedicated to Oscar Wilde (number 34), John Singer Sargent (number 31), and Augustus John (number 33). Turn right on to the Embankment and a few yards along is **Cheyne Walk**. These splendid houses were on the water's edge until the reclamation of the Embankment in the 19th century. Blue plaques mark the former homes of pre-Raphaelite painter Dante Gabriel Rosetti as well as the author George Eliot.

Perhaps the most famous Chelsea resident of all was Sir Thomas More, who settled by the riverside in 1523. A plaque some hundred yards up Beaufort Street marks the site of his house. In 1535 he was taken by boat to trial at Westminster and eventually beheaded on Tower Hill for refusing to accept the Oath of Supremacy, by which Henry VIII claimed himself equal to God. Sir Thomas intended **All Saints Church** (off Cheyne Walk) to be his final resting place, but his tomb is actually filled by his wife, Alice, as his head was taken to Canterbury. A modern statue in front of the church honours the man who declared on the scaffold, "I die the King's good servant, but God's first."

Hampstead

Hampstead is the most glorious of central London's villages and has long been home to artists and intellectuals. Byron, Keats, H.G. Wells, Robert Louis Stevenson, D.H. Lawrence, and John Constable all lived here.

The chief glory of Hampstead is the 324 hectares (800 acre) **Hampstead Heath**, which has attracted Londoners in search of fresh air and relaxation since the 16th century. Kite-flying on Parliament Hill is a popular pastime. The centre of the village is full of lovely narrow lanes with immaculately tended houses and gardens. Three that are open to the public are: the **Freud Museum**, on Maresfield Gardens, the home of the father of psychoanalysis; **Keats' House**, on Keats Grove, now a museum dedicated to the tragic poet; and **Fenton House**, a 17th-century building

with fine furniture, works of art, and early musical in-
struments. Much of Hampstead's charm lies in the small details that are easy to miss (a blue plaque here, a hidden
garden of someone famous there) so the best way to see it is
on a guided walking tour.

To the north of the Heath is **Kenwood House**, one of the
most important country houses in the capital. It was remodelled in 1764 by Robert Adam, and the superb architecture
and its magnificent collection of paintings (Rembrandt, Turner, Gainsborough) are worth the trip to Hampstead alone.
What's more, entrance is free. The outdoor summer concerts
in the idyllic setting by the lake are a highlight of the London
social calendar.

To the east of Hampstead Heath is London's most famous
last resting place, **Highgate Cemetery**. To visit the overgrown romantic western section you must join one of the
hour-long tours, which depart on the hour. The most famous
grave, that of Karl Marx, lies in the less interesting modern
eastern section.

Greenwich

Greenwich has such a grand maritime history that the most
appropriate (and most enjoyable) way to reach it is by
boat either from Charing Cross Pier, Tower Pier, or Westminster Pier. The twin domes of the Royal Naval College
frame the white cube of the Queen's House with the sloping
lawns of Greenwich Park beyond.

Hard by the pier rise the tall and graceful masts of the
Cutty Sark—climb aboard to explore the last of the British
sailing clippers, now in dry dock. Adjacent to the *Cutty Sark*
is the diminutive *Gipsy Moth IV,* in which Sir Francis Chich-
ester became the first Englishman to sail around the world
single-handed in 1966.

It's an uphill climb from the pier to the **Old Royal Observatory**. The complex takes in Flamsteed House, a Wren building of 1675 which housed several Astronomer Royals and their equipment. As England's most important naval observation site, Greenwich became the world's zero meridian of longitude in 1884. The observatory ceased to function in the 1930s when smog and city lights forced it out into the Sussex countryside, and the building now houses a museum.

The **National Maritime Museum** is the world's largest museum of its kind. If it floats, or ever floated, you'll find it here. There is too much to take in all in one visit, but don't miss the Neptune Hall and the Barge House, where full-size craft include an 18th-century royal barge. The **Royal Naval College** occupies the Baroque buildings of the Royal Naval Hospital (until 1869 a maritime version of the Royal Hospital Chelsea; see page 55). Both Prince Andrew and Prince Charles attended this training school for naval officers. You can visit the Grand Hall and the Chapel (afternoons only, closed Thursday).

There is plenty more to see in Greenwich: the **Fan Museum**, the 17th-century **Ranger's House**, and the excellent **weekend market**. Join a guided tour, setting off from the Tourist Information Centre between noon and 2:00 P.M.

Boats leave regularly from Greenwich for the 25-minute trip to the **Thames Barrier**. As you head downriver, the salty tang of the sea may hit you and you realize that the Thames, with its industrial landscape of smokestacks and cranes, is still a working river. It can also be a lethal force, as it last proved in 1953 when 14 people were drowned in their basements as far upstream as Westminster. To ensure London would never be flooded again, the £450 million Thames Barrier was built between 1975 and 1982. An audiovisual presentation explains how it works and tours show you the Barrier close up.

PARKS AND GARDENS

Within a 10 km (6-mile) radius of Piccadilly Circus, some 80 parks, gardens, commons, and heaths cover a quarter of inner London's total area. While ornamental gateways, formal flower beds, and monumental statuary adorn some of these open spaces (particularly the royal parks) others, such as Hampstead Heath, have been left in a natural state.

Hyde Park is probably the best known of the royal parks due to its central location, its size (138 hectares/340 acres) and its visitor attractions. At the Marble Arch corner of the park is **Speakers' Corner**. Historically this is the point where mass demonstrations used to take place, and a right of free assembly was granted here. Sunday morning is when soapbox orators spout their stuff. They may wax lyrical on philosophy, religion, politics, or anything else as long as it isn't treasonable, racist, or likely to cause a breach of the peace.

When you tire of lending your ears, take a boat out on the **Serpentine** (Hyde Park's man-made lake), or take the plunge in the Lido, the part of the Serpentine reserved for hardy swimmers. At one time Kensington Gardens were separated from Hyde Park by a wall. Nowadays the two merge imperceptibly. Temporary exhibitions of modern art are held at the Serpentine Gallery (tel. 0171-402 6075), while traditionalists, especially with children, will probably be more interested in the lovingly worn statue of **Peter Pan**. A very different statue lies to the south of the park. The **Albert Memorial** stands at 53 metres (175 feet) and commemorates Queen Victoria's beloved German consort, whose untimely death she mourned for nearly forty years.

St. James's Park is the oldest and the most ornamental of the royal parks. It hasn't always been a pleasant place, however. The site was once occupied by St. James's Hospital

Dusk on the Serpentine—take a leisurely row on Hyde Park's man-made lake.

(from where the park takes its name), once surrounded by swampland where the hospital's last inmates—13 young leper women—fed their hogs.

Walk the length of the park from Horse Guards to Buckingham Palace and pause on the bridge in the centre of the lake. To the east are the domes and towers of Whitehall, to the west is the Palace—a magical view either way. The bird sanctuary on Duck Island is home to exotic waterfowl and pelicans (a legacy of a pair presented to Charles II by the Russian ambassador in 1665).

If you would like a break from the crowds and some fresh air after visiting Madame Tussaud's, adjacent **Regent's Park** is the perfect tonic. The elegant white stuccoed buildings bordering the park were designed by the Prince Regent's architect, John Nash, and laid out during the 1820s.

They are undoubtedly the most elegant example of town planning in central London. None of the park's buildings are open to the public, but some of their exteriors are the finest in London—don't miss Cumberland Terrace.

There are many attractions in the park. You can take a boat on the lake, play tennis, or enjoy the heady fragrance of summer roses in Queen Mary's Gardens. The adjacent **Open-Air Theatre** is a delightful place to watch Shakespeare under the stars on a balmy summer evening. If you would like to reach the park by water, **narrowboats** ply the Regent's Canal from Little Venice (by Warwick Avenue underground station) and are a very pleasant way to travel to the park on a fine day. Alternatively you can walk along the towpath.

MUSEUMS AND GALLERIES

On a first visit you can't hope to do more than scratch the surface of London's cultural wealth. The sheer size of the major museums is as awesome as the total number of collections open to the public.

Admission to most of the larger institutions is no longer free, but the British Museum, the National Gallery, the National Portrait Gallery, and the Tate Gallery are notable exceptions (even these, however, change admission to special exhibitions). The museums and galleries described below all fall within the small central "tourist London" area, but step slightly off the beaten track and you will discover many of the less well-known collections, some of which are mentioned in the section in this chapter on London's Villages, pages 53-58.

Global Collections

The unique **British Museum** on Great Russell Street opened to the public in 1759, although the present building dates from 1823. Within its 7 hectares (17½ acres) it holds one of the largest and finest collections of antiquities in the world, magnificent medieval treasures, and many of the world's oldest and most famous documents and books. Extensive as the museum is, its collections are continually expanding — a recent addition is the Weston Gallery of Roman Britain, documenting 400 years of Roman occupation.

For an introductory tour either take one of the museum's own guided tours, or seek out the highlights listed below, in the following order.

Assyrian Sculptures and Reliefs—The Khorsabad Entrance (Rooms 16-17). A colossal gateway from 710 B.C. complete with huge, human-headed winged bulls and magnificent stone panels depicting hunting scenes, is the highlight of what is considered to be the greatest collection of Assyrian sculptures in the world.

Elgin Marbles (Room 8). These friezes and figures from the Parthenon in Athens are the single most famous exhibit in the museum. The detail on them is perfect and they count as one of the great masterpieces of Classical Art.

Rosetta Stone (Room 25). This tablet of black basalt, discovered in 1799, was the first key to deciphering hieroglyphics. Egyptologists will also appreciate the magnificent statuary in this area.

Egyptian Mummies (in Rooms 60-61). Possibly the most popular section of the whole museum, and a must for children. Within these rooms there are not only mummified humans, but also sacred mummified animals, which range vastly in size from a shrew to a small bull.

Sutton Hoo Treasure (in Room 41). A glittering treasure trove from the burial ship of an ancient English king, dating from around A.D. 625, and found at Sutton Hoo in Suffolk in 1939.

The Manuscript Saloon (Room 30) and King's Library (Room 32). If you have ever wondered what the handwriting

The British Museum on Great Russell Street holds one of the finest collections of antiquities in the world.

of such greats as Michelangelo, Leonardo da Vinci, and Beethoven looked like, this is your chance to find out. Some of the world's oldest and most famous books are here, including two of the four original copies of the Magna Carta, a Gutenburg bible from 1453, and Shakespeare's First Folio, dating from 1623.

Other areas with great and popular treasures include the Mausoleum of Halicarnassus (Room 12), the Babylonian Room (Room 54), Prints and Drawings (Room 67), Celtic Britain (Room 37), Roman Britain (Rooms 35 and 40), the Medieval Gallery (Room 42), Clocks and Watches (Room 44), and the Portland Vase (Room 70). Every hour on the hour during weekday afternoons, a brief glimpse is allowed of the magnificent domed **Reading Room** where several greats have studied, among them Karl Marx, who worked on *Das Kapital* here.

The **Victoria and Albert Museum** (on Cromwell Road, SW7) houses one of the most comprehensive collections of fine and applied arts in the world. Its 13 km (8 miles) of corridors and 5 hectares (12 acres) of galleries might seem

The V&A is one of the world's largest treasure troves of fine and applied art.

daunting, but for those who stick with it, it can be highly rewarding. Take a free guided tour to get you started.

The following collections and exhibits are just some of the highlights at the V&A: European Art up to 1600; Continental European Art from 1600–1900; Northern Renaissance and Spanish Art; Arts of Asia; The Constable Collection, The Cast Courts; The Dress Collection; Frank Lloyd Wright Gallery.

Admission to the V&A is free, but you are asked at the entrance to make a suggested donation of £3.50 per adult. There is no further charge for gallery tours, which depart at regular times Monday to Saturday, and at 3:00 P.M. on Sunday.

Next to the V&A is the **Science Museum** (Exhibition Road, SW7), founded after the Great Exhibition of 1851. If the V&A is a traditional "look, don't touch" museum, the Science Museum is very much the opposite. Many of the wonders of science are literally within your grasp as you push a button here or pull a lever there. However, with exhibits as impressive as *Puffing Billy* (the oldest surviving locomotive in the world), Stephenson's famous *Rocket*, Amy Johnson's *Gipsy Moth,* and *Apollo 10*, just looking is also a pleasure.

The fascinating **Wellcome Museum of the History of Medicine** on the top floor justifies the entrance fee to the Science Museum alone. Leave the children at **Launch Pad**, where there are dozens of fascinating experiments for budding young Einsteins, while you learn about trepanning and

A Triceratops greets visitors to the Natural History Museum, where one may also behold a life-size model of a whale.

other tribal medicine techniques which will make your hair stand on end.

The adjacent **Natural History Museum** (Cromwell Road, SW7) completes this extraordinary concentration of learning. As in the case of Science Museum, it too has become "hands-on," and its newest gallery is devoted to ecological issues. Your abiding memories, however, are likely to be of the building itself—an awesome, terracotta, Romanesque "cathedral," and of its largest inhabitants: a life-size model of a blue whale measuring nearly 28 metres (93 feet) long, and dinosaur skeletons towering up to 5 metres (16 feet) above you.

The **Museum of Mankind** (Burlington Gardens, near Piccadilly) delves into the most remote corners of the world to chart ethnic societies, and an enigmatic Easter Island statue greets you in the foyer. This is actually the British Museum's ethnography department and it draws on its parent's vast wealth for both long-term changing exhibitions and permanent items. The end result is always colourful and very educational.

London Calling

Students of London history should make a point of fitting the excellent **Museum of London** (London Wall, the Barbican) into their itinerary. The well-presented modern galleries chart every aspect of the capital from its beginnings as *Londinium* to the present. See a section of Roman Wall, a plague bell, the old door of Newgate Prison, and the Lord Mayor's gilded State Coach.

The **London Transport Museum** is housed in Covent Garden's old flower market and is a delight for both young (for hands-on fun) and old (for nostalgia). You can see London's first omnibus (it was horse-drawn) and some of the world's first underground carriages and trains. A simulator allows you to take the driving seat in an underground train along the Circle line.

The World's a Stage

Several important new museums have opened recently to chronicle Britain's rich entertainment heritage. The most traditional is the **Theatre Museum**, located in the heart of Covent Garden next to the London Transport Museum. Dedicated to all aspects of the performing arts, it has a fascinating array of props, stage models, costumes, prints, and posters.

The **Museum of the Moving Image** (MOMI) in the South Bank Centre has rapidly established itself as a London visitors' favourite. Not only does it have an extensive collection of memorabilia, but it is also London's most interactive museum, where costumed actor-guides tell how everything works. They will even help you to fly like Superman or read the news from an autocue.

WW II fighter planes at the Imperial War Museum.

Shakespeare's Globe Theatre has been reconstructed on Bankside, just east of its original site. Performances are held in the open-air theatre throughout the summer, and a fascinating museum is open year-round to tell the story of the original theatre and its faithful reconstruction using 450-year-old methods.

The BBC Experience in Bradcasting House on Portland Place tells the whole story of the excellent British Broacast Corporation in many fun ways—visitors, for instance, can watch vintage clips or even produce a radio show.

War (and Peace)

The **Imperial War Museum** (Lambeth Road on the South Bank) is widely acknowledged as home of one of London's finest collections. It deals with 20th-century conflict involving British troops, and treats the delicate subject of war high-

The National Gallery's collection has grown from its original 38 paintings (in 1824) to now include over 2,000 works.

ly commendably. Exhibits are often dramatically displayed (aircraft are suspended in a huge glass atrium), and interactive and multi-sensory displays recreate sights, sounds, and emotions of war.

The **National Army Museum** (Royal Hospital Road, Chelsea) goes back beyond this century to the formation of the British Army in 1485. This traditional museum holds many interesting relics and trophies, including the skeleton of Napoleon's horse, the handwritten order for the ill-fated Charge of the Light Brigade and, right up to date, Gulf War memorabilia.

Three other museums with appeal to those who are curious about life during wartime but do not want to see displays of battle flags and uniforms are: **H.M.S. *Belfast*** (moored opposite the Tower of London; see page 39); **Florence Nightingale Museum** (St. Thomas' Hospital, Lambeth Palace Road, on the South Bank opposite the Houses of Parliament); and the **Cabinet War Rooms** (King Charles Street off Whitehall—see page 29). H.M.S. *Belfast* is as much about life at sea during peacetime as during war, while the

award-winning museum dedicated to the world's most famous nurse shows how she developed modern nursing techniques during the hell of the Crimean War. The Cabinet War
Rooms are an atmospheric bunker from which Churchill
helped to inspire Britain to reach its "finest hour."

The Britain at War Experience (on Tooley Street near
the London Bridge underground stop) vividly re-creates the
world wars as experienced by the British; spectators crouch
in a shelter at the sound of the air-raid siren, dodge debris,
and in other ways relive Britain's finest hour.

The Best of the Rest

The **Wallace Collection** (at Hertford House, Manchester
Square), tucked away behind Selfridges on Oxford Street, is
probably London's best-kept artistic secret. It's both a museum
and an art gallery, and features 18th-century French furniture
(with pieces from Marie Antoinette's apartments at Versailles),
exquisite Sèvres porcelain, and contemporary paintings by
Watteau, Fragonard, and Boucher. Alongside works by Rembrandt, Titian, Velázquez, and Rubens sits one of the world's
favourite paintings, the *Laughing Cavalier* by Frans Hals.

Sir John Soane's Museum (13 Lincoln's Inn Fields,
WC2) holds several famous Hogarth paintings (including
The Rake's Progress series) plus works by Turner and
Canaletto. Soane was a prominent late 18th-century London
architect and his fascinating house has been kept precisely
how he left it.

The innovative and ambitious **Design Museum** (at the
far end of Butler's Wharf, next to Tower Bridge) features
the very latest designs that mass production has to offer—
some still on the drawing board, others already in production. In more traditional museum fashion, exhibits chroni-
cling the development of the design of such familiar

The Lady of Shallot by J. W. Waterhouse at the Tate Gallery.

household items as the telephone or vacuum cleaner are surprisingly fascinating.

Great Art Houses

 From a group of 38 paintings purchased for the nation in 1824, the **National Gallery** in Trafalgar Square has grown to include over 2,000 works and is one of the finest collections of Western European art in the world.

The collection is divided into four colour-coded sections: the Sainsbury Wing, the West Wing, the North Wing, and the East Wing. Within each section the paintings are arranged by school.

To the west of the main building, the Sainsbury Wing (added in 1990), houses painting from 1260 to 1510, including Leonardo da Vinci's *Virgin of the Rocks*, Uccello's *The Battle of San Romano,* Raphael's *Cruxifixion,* and Botticelli's *Venus and Mars*.

The West Wing, to the left of the main entrance on Trafalgar Square, contains paintings from 1510 to 1600, including as Titian's *Bacchus and Ariadne* and Holbein the Younger's *The Ambassadors*. Paintings from 1600 to 1700 are exhibited in the North Wing (access is from Orange Street or via central hall). Rubens' *Le Chapeau de Paille*, Veláquez' *The Toilet of Venus*, Rembrandt's *Self Portrait*, Jan Van Eyck's *Giovanni Arnolfini and his Wife*, and Caravaggio's *Supper at Eumaeus* are all housed in this section.

The East Wing, to the right of the main entrance, covers art from 1700 to 1920. English works are represented here by Constable's *Hay Wain*, Gainsborough's *Mr. and Mrs. Andrew*, Turner's *Rain, Steam, and Speed*, and *The Fighting Téméraire*. Impressionists in this section include Monet's *Water Lily Pond*, Van Gogh's *Cornfield with Cypresses*, *Sunflowers*, Cezanne's *Bathers*, and Renoir's *Parapluies*.

Free hour-long tours of the gallery are conducted twice daily in winter; three times daily in summer (except Sunday). The Micro Gallery in the Sainsbury Wing also houses a computerized information system which enables you to assemble your own tour.

For information about special exhibitions, films, lecture tours etc. telephone 071-839 3321 (071-839 3526 for recorded information).

The **National Portrait Gallery** (off Charing Cross, directly behind the National Gallery) was founded in 1856 as a "Gallery of the Portraits of the most eminent persons in British History." Despite this rather worthy description, it is fun to see what medieval kings and queens and personalities such as Chaucer, Pepys, and Nell Gwynn really looked like. The collection is also right up to date, with portraits of Mick Jagger, Bob Geldof, and the present royal family.

The **Tate Gallery** (on the river at Millbank, a short walk from Parliament Square) is home to the **National Collection of Modern Art** (British and foreign works) and the **National Collection of British Historic Painting** (dating from the 16th century). Some of the highlights of the British collection include Constable's famous views of Salisbury Cathedral, Joshua Reynold's portraits, Hogarth's acerbic commentaries on 18th- century low life, Stubbs' landscape and sporting scenes, Gainsborough's portraits and naturalistic landscapes, and the romantic epics of the pre-Raphaelite Group.

The Clore Gallery (an extension of the main building) was purpose built to hold the huge Turner catalogue, which includes 282 oil paintings and more than 20,000 other works by the Covent Garden-born artist. The Modern Art section features several Henry Moore sculptures, Cubism by Picasso and Braque, Surrealism by Dali and Magritte, and Pop Art by Andy Warhol.

Children can ride camels, llamas, and ponies at the Zoo.

The **Courtauld Institute Galleries** at Somerset House on the Strand provides a superb crash course in art history. The collection features 14th-, 15th-, and 16th-century religious masterpieces, 17th-century Italian art, 20th-century British art, and key works by Rubens, Cranach, Brueghel ,and Botticelli. The two rooms into which everyone crowds, however, house the **Impressionists and Post-Impressionists**: here you will find Manet's *Bar at the Folies-Bergère* and a sketch for *Déjeuner sur l'Herbe*; *La Loge* by Renoir; Van Gogh's *Self-Portrait with Bandaged Ear;* and *Nevermore* by Gauguin.

There are two other very important traditional art galleries in central London, the **Queen's Gallery** (see page 23) and the **Royal Academy of Arts** (see page 44). Both show temporary exhibitions, which are always avidly anticipated by art lovers. Modern Art fans should look to see what's on at the **Hayward Gallery** (South Bank Centre) and the **Barbican Art Gallery**.

CHILDREN'S LONDON

A capital city can be a daunting place to take a child, but with the diversity of children's attractions and the number of parks in London, you should never be too hard pushed to keep the little ones amused. In addition to the attractions listed below, which cater specifically for children, the majority of even London's most august institutions provide more and more for children, with museum trails and interactive exhibits.

Old Friends

Call it kitsch, call it corny, but the queues still don't seem to be getting any shorter at **Madame Tussaud's**, which has been packing them in at the present site on Marylebone Road since 1884. Evergreens include Henry VIII and his six wives and the present British royal family. The famous **Chamber of Horrors** is always guaranteed to chill, with no

shortage of modern monsters to carry on the grisly tradition of Jack the Ripper and Doctor Crippen. A combined ticket is available for star-gazing in the London Planetarium next door (see page 76).

London Zoo, a short walk across Regent's Park, has long been a firm favourite with children. Highlights include the aviary, the insect and arachnid house, and Moonlight World, where you can watch nocturnal animals at work.

The H.M.S. Belfast, now a floating museum, led the bombardment of the Normandy Coast on D-Day.

Blood and Thunder

The "horrors" of Madame Tussaud's seem like mere pranks in comparison with some of the goings on at the **London Dungeon**. Set deep in spooky, dark, dripping vaults beneath London Bridge, the world's first medieval horror museum is not for the sensitive. Needless to say, older children love the wax tableaux—graphic portrayals of such quaint old English customs as the rack, execution by boiling in water (sanctioned of course by Henry VIII), and hanging, drawing (disembowelling), and quartering. Not for the faint-hearted!

At the **Tower of London** the keen sense of history evoked by the beefeaters with their picture-book costumes and colourful stories, plus the wonderful exhibits and ancient buildings, fascinate children and adults (see pages 39-42).

Children keen on military hardware will enjoy the exhibits and multi-sensory experiences at the **Imperial War Museum** (see page 67), while scrambling up and down the ladders and along the decks of **H.M.S.** *Belfast* (see page 42) is a young explorer's dream.

One of London's newest children's attractions is a game called **Quasar**, where sixteen players split into two teams and battle with laser guns through a futuristic, smoky, nuclear reactor-type structure on three levels. Parents with pacific tendencies may not approve, but teenagers love it. You will find it in the Trocadero at Piccadilly Circus, a noisy centre where the style of shops and computer and simulator games make you feel past it if you are over 25. The **Guinness World of Records** here is a good all-round family attraction.

Child's Play

If beheading and loud bangs are not your cup of tea, don't worry, there are three excellent traditional children's toys and games museums.

The biggest is the **Bethnal Green Museum of Childhood**, which claims to be the largest public collection of dolls' houses, games, and puppets on view anywhere in the world (closed Fridays). It is located slightly out of the centre of London, a short walk from Bethnal Green underground station. By contrast **Pollock's Toy Museum** (1 Scala Street, W1) is a mere toy box housed in two small adjoining houses dating from 1760. Visiting it is a bit like stumbling upon childhood memories in granny's attic, and is one of London's most charming places. The **London Toy and Model Museum** (Craven Hill Road, Paddington) boasts the biggest collection of model trains in

Europe and is a great favourite with dads! It's best to visit on Sunday mornings when the only regular steam service left in London carries passengers around the garden.

For really fabulous toys to take home as gifts, the ultimate place to shop is **Hamley's** in Regent Street. This is the world's largest toy store and it's always very busy, so don't expect a quick visit. Covent Garden is excellent for small, high-quality craft and toy shops, and the bus-kers here will keep the whole family amused.

Rock'n'Roll

Almost all teenagers will want to head straight for the **Hard Rock Café** to indulge in a burger and chips, hear loud music, see the rock and roll memorabilia on the walls, and take home the ubiquitous T-shirt. Now into its third decade, the Hard Rock is still massively popular so be prepared for a wait to be seated (see page 141).

The London Planetarium, just next to Madame Tussaud's, stages Laserium shows, where laser pyrotechnics perform to a pounding beat. The latest state-of-the-art attraction by the Madame Tussaud's organization is **Rock Circus** (at the London Pavilion, Piccadilly Circus). Short-wave headphones pick up the music as you walk past static wax figures of rock heroes and the rousing finale is a show which features bionic/audio-animatronic models of some of the world's greatest rock musicians, past and present.

DAY TRIPS

London's best-loved short day trips all lie within 34 km (21 miles) of the centre of town: the Royal Botanic Gardens at Kew is 11 km (7 miles) away, but still on the underground line (Kew Gardens); Hampton Court Palace is at 23 km (14 miles), by British Rail from Waterloo or

Green Line bus; Windsor, 40 km (25 miles) by British Rail from Paddington or Waterloo or by Green Line bus. Package tours may cram two, or even all three, of these into one day, but try to resist the temptation. Each can make a day out in its own right, with riverside pubs, tearooms, restaurants, and quaint shops, as well as leafy surroundings, to enjoy at your leisure.

The Royal Botanic Gardens, Kew

These famous gardens were founded in 1759 by Princess Augusta (mother of George III) and laid out by that legendary gardener Lancelot "Capability" Brown.

A combination of research centre and public pleasure gardens, they cover over 116 hectares (288 acres) and contain over 25,000 species and varieties of plant. There are three primary glasshouses to visit—the **Princess of Wales Conservatory**, representing modern Kew, the **Palm House,** and the **Temperate House**, the latter two being magnificent Victorian crystal palaces. **Kew Palace**, near the main gate, is the smallest of all the royal palaces in England. The **Orangerie**, built in 1761, now houses a gift shop and restaurant.

Wax statues of pop stars Annie Lennox and Jimi Hendrix wave to passersby from the London Pavilion in Piccadilly Circus.

Windsor Castle

Windsor Castle is the same vintage as the Tower of London, and is one of a circle of forts built by William the Conqueror, one day's march from London. The royal standard flies when the Sovereign is in residence, and there is a Changing of the Guard ceremony at 11:00 A.M.

Picturesque in the extreme, the world's largest occupied castle sprawls on top of a bluff with a commanding view over the Thames. The walled precinct divides into lower, middle, and upper wards, and are dominated by the chess-piece Round Tower, built in 1170. Additions were made piecemeal through the centuries, in particular St. George's Chapel(1478–1511) and the luxurious State Apartments.

St. George's Chapel is the architectural *tour de force* of the castle. This fine example of the Perpendicular style ranks on a par with the Henry VII Chapel in Westminster Abbey.

The other glory of the castle is the **State Apartments**, decorated with carved and gilded furniture from France and England, Gobelins tapestries, masterpieces by Rubens and van Dyck, and ceiling scenes by Antonio Verrio. The State Apartments are closed when the Queen is in Official Residence, from March to early May, most of June, and over Christmas and the New Year.

Finally, don't miss the incredible **Queen Mary's Dolls' House**. It was designed by Sir Edwin Lutyens, and its contents include real Wedgwood china, a tiny working Hoover, and functioning lighting and plumbing. Next door to the Doll's House is the Exhibition of Drawings by such masters as Holbein, Leonardo da Vinci, and Michelangelo.

The streets below the castle have more than their fair share of cheap touristy shops and mediocre restaurants, and in summer become very crowded. Escape across the bridge to **Eton**, where the famous elite public (i.e., private) school has been in existence for more than 550 years, producing no less than 20 British Prime Ministers. Enquire at the tourist information office (near Windsor and Eton Central railway station) about tours of the school.

Windsor's other main tourist attraction (also by Central railway station) is **Royalty & Empire**, where the Madame Tussaud's Group use all their expertise in static tableaux and moving bionics to bring alive Queen Victoria's Diamond Jubilee celebrations of 1897.

The royal seat of kings since William the Conqueror, Windsor Castle symbolizes England's proud history.

Hampton Court Palace

This beautiful red-brick Tudor mansion lies 23 km (14 miles) west of central London. It is undoubtably the most romantic of London's royal palaces, and the majority of it is open to the general public.

Built in 1514 for Cardinal Wolsey, it was appropriated by Henry VIII in 1525, following Wolsey's fall from grace. It was Henry's favourite palace, and he spent five of his six honeymoons here. You enter through the Great Gatehouse (built during the 1530s), which leads on to Base Court and Anne Boleyn's Gateway. On the inside is a magnificent astronomical clock made for King Henry VIII in 1540. It shows the hour, day, month, phases of the Moon, and even the state of the tides.

The **State Apartments** are some of the most sumptuous of any royal palace, featuring works by such great and gifted craftsmen as Grinling Gibbons, Antonio Verrio, and William Kent. Wolsey's Closet is a remarkably well-preserved study lined with delicate linenfold wooden panelling. The highlights, however, are the **Great Hall** and the **Chapel Royal**.

The grounds are also of great interest. The rare **Royal Tennis Court**, built for King James I in 1626, is still in frequent use, and games of royal tennis may be watched here. In appearance it is a cross between squash and lawn tennis, played on an indoor court. Wait for a break and ask one of the players to explain the basic rules of the game. Royal (sometimes corrupted to real) tennis was all the rage among the European aristocracy during the 16th century.

The Hampton Court Palace was a favourite of Henry VIII. He spent five of his six honeymoons here.

If you would like to keep the children amused for an hour or two, take them to the famous **Maze**, which has been baffling royalty and visitors for some 300 years. The paths within the maze wind around and around for almost a kilometre (about half a mile).

WHAT TO DO

No city offers more in the way of leisure pursuits than London, beginning with some of the world's best shopping.

SHOPPING

There is so much variety and so much style in London that the rich fly here just for the shops. London is still pretty well free of large indoor malls, so on most occasions you will have to brave the elements.

Where to Shop

Start in the West End, if only for some reconnoitering of the covered arcades and elegant department stores. If it's antiques,

Covent Garden has endless attractions for shoppers, including trendy shops and plenty of places to eat.

fine art, jewellery, leather goods, or top-quality clothing you are after, wander down Bond Street and on to Piccadilly, Regent, and Jermyn Streets. If you want more down-to-earth goods at more down-to-earth prices, Oxford Street is home to the big department stores. Look in Marks & Spencer for good quality clothing at moderate prices. The comprehensive Self-ridges offers top-quality one-stop shopping.

Knightsbridge is the biggest challenge to the West End. The emphasis is on high fashion along Sloane Street and Beauchamp Place, while Harrods dominates Brompton Road and sets the pace, and style of customer, for the immediate surrounding area. Chelsea offers the trendsetting King's Road plus Fulham Road chic. Kensington High Street proves only slightly less frenetic than Oxford Street, while Kensington Church Street is a haven for antique seekers.

When to Shop

Most shops open from 9:00–9:30 A.M. to 5:30–6:00 P.M. Monday to Saturday, though some Mayfair shops close on Saturday afternoon. Traditionally there is late-night shopping in Knights-bridge on Wednesday until 7:00 P.M. and in Oxford Street and Regent Street on Thursday until 7:30–8 P.M. In practice, however, shops are opening longer and longer hours. Covent Garden shops have always kept late hours, most of them staying open from 10:00 A.M. to 8:00 P.M. Monday to Saturday—many open on Sunday afternoon, too. Serious bargain hunters descend on London for the sales in January and July, although these days many stores have sales on an almost permanent basis.

Street Markets

If you want to catch the real flavour of London shopping and some of its most colourful characters, then you should head for one of the city's many street markets.

Portobello Road (Notting Hill) is always popular; antiques, bric-a-brac, and miscellaneous bargains on Saturday, and fruit and vegetables on weekdays (closed Tuesday).

Petticoat Lane (Middlesex Street, in the East End) is the place for shopping on Sunday and has a wide variety of goods, including lots of leather. Adjacent is the even more colourful, and chaotic, **Brick Lane Market**, where second-hand bargains abound and the spirit of the old Cockney East End and the flavour of the new Asian East End collide.

Covent Garden's **Jubilee Market** is popular with both tourists and locals. Antiques on Monday, crafts, clothes, and food Tuesday to Friday, and hand-made crafts at the weekend.

There are two north London markets that are well worth exploring. **Camden Passage** at Islington (Wednesdays and Saturdays for antiques and Thursdays for books, prints, and drawings) is set in the courtyard of a permanent established antique centre. **Camden Lock Market**, just north of Regent's Park, is a youthful weekend market for arts and crafts, antiques, bric-a-brac, health foods, and jewellery.

The **New Caledonian Market** at Bermondsey Square (near London Bridge) is the place for serious antique collectors. The dealers are here before trading starts at 5:00 or 6:00 A.M. each Friday, and by breakfast time the best bargains have gone.

For a comprehensive list of street markets ask at tourist information offices for their brochure "Markets in London."

Best Buys

Antiques. It's easy to be fooled, so look for the seal of the professional associations LAPADA and BADA. If you find formal antique shopping a little intimidating try market centres such as Alfie's Antique Market (Church Street, Marylebone), Gray's Market (Davies Street, next to Bond Street underground station), Bond Street Antique Centre (New Bond

Street), or Antiquarius, Chenil Galleries, and Chelsea Antique Market (all three on King's Road).

Books. Charing Cross Road is a mecca for second-hand and rare volumes and here you will also find Foyle's, London's largest, though not necessarily the most efficient, bookshop. Waterstone's next door may be a better bet. Dillon's on Gower Street andHatchard's on Piccadilly are two other good bookshops.

Clothing. Savile Row and St. James's fill most upper-crust masculine requirements from head (a bowler hat at Lock's) to toe (hand-made shoes at Lobb's). King's Road, Covent Garden, South Molton Street, and St. Christopher's Place (both off Oxford Street) and Knightsbridge are for the stylish, while those in search of good-quality, typically British garb, need go no farther than Marks & Spencer (Oxford Street and branches) or, particularly for woollens, the Scotch House (Knightsbridge and branches).

Fabrics. Branches of John Lewis (including Peter Jones on Sloane Square) have a good everyday range but Liberty's are world famous for their prints and it is always a pleasure to visit their beautiful, galleried Regent Street store.

Fine Foods. For a traditional taste of England go to Fortnum and Mason or Harrods. For tea it would be hard to beat Twining's on the Strand, who have been providing Londoners with their "Rosie Lee" since 1717. Cheese lovers will be spoilt for choice at the rustic Neal's Yard Dairy (Covent Garden) or by the 300-plus varieties on offer at Paxton & Whitfield, London's oldest cheese shop, on Jermyn Street.

Perfumes. Stay on Jermyn Street for altogether sweeter smells at Floris, purveyors of perfume since 1730. Penhaligon's at Wellington Street, Covent Garden, also specializes in traditional English toiletries.

Rainwear. You will probably need some protection from the elements while in London, so why not go native and keep dry in style in the famous red and beige check of Burberry's on Haymarket?

Tobacco. St. James's, not surprisingly, is the place to go. Dunhill and Fribourg & Tryer both carry pipe mixtures and the very best imported cigars.

SPORTS

The British have always been a sporty race and Londoners are no exception. There's horse riding and swimming in Hyde Park, sailing and windsurfing in Docklands, and many of London's parks (including Regent's Park) offer cheap public tennis courts. There's not much room to swing a golf club in central London but get out to Richmond Park and only the deer will complain if you hook or slice. Whatever sport you want to participate in, call Sportsline on 0171-222 8000 for free information.

When it comes to spectator sports, Londoners (like all Brits) enjoy **football** (soccer). Between 20,000 and 40,000 supporters turn out each Saturday to see the likes of Arsenal, Tottenham Hotspur (Spurs) or Chelsea. Look in the national papers on a Saturday morning or any of the London listings magazines to see who's playing.

The **rugby** season runs from September to April. Twickenham is the main venue for amateur Rugby Union matches (tel. 0181-892 8161). The Rugby League finals take place in May at Wembley Stadium (tel. 0181-900 1234). Local games are held throughout London, and are listed in the Saturday edition of all national newspapers.

Alternatively, during the summer you can opt for a genteel game of **cricket** at Lord's (St. John's Wood, tel. 0171-289 1611) or the Oval (Kennington, tel. 0171-582 6660).

Tennis comes to London in a big way during the Wimbledon warm-up tournament at the Queen's Club, Baron's Court, followed by the big one at the All England Club, Wimbledon. You can queue for the outside courts for the early rounds but overnight queueing is necessary for the latter stages. That is, unless, of course, you have been successful in the ticket ballot—send a stamped, self-addressed envelope to the All England Lawn Tennis Club, Church Road, Wimbledon SW19 5AE some months in advance for details; call 081-946-2244 for more informaion.

Horse racing is the sport of royalty and the very rich. You can watch the thoroughbreds—often including some of the Queen's own horses—run at Ascot and Epsom, both within easy reach of London.

Tennis at its best—it's not impossible to find a seat at Wimbledon, but it's not easy.

By contrast, **greyhound racing** is the working man's game. There are seven stadiums around London where races are held year round, including those at Wembley and Wimbledon. It's an evening event and you can combine dinner with the dogs at most tracks.

ENTERTAINMENT

More goes on in London in a day than in a year in most places. Just try reading all the reviews and events in the London listings magazines for a single week.

For many visitors to London the **theatre** is what makes the city special by night. There are some 43 functioning mainstream theatres in central London alone. Most of these are in the West End, staging popular comedies, musicals, and dramas. The top-quality exceptions are the National Theatre at the South Bank Centre, which stages innovative productions of the classics and the best modern pieces; the Old Vic (next to Waterloo station), which specializes in revivals of the classics; the Royal Court Theatre on Sloane Square, Chelsea, famous for drama; the Royal Shakespeare Company at the Barbican; Shakespeare's New Globe Theatre on Bankside, which stages works by the Bard and other playwrights in a faithful reconstruction of the original theatre during summer months.

In addition to the big West End theatres there are dozens of excellent suburban playhouses, and summer outdoor theatre is performed in Regent's Park and Holland Park, west of Kensington. There is also a large and proliferating number of fringe venues where you can see experimental and offbeat works for a fraction of the price of a West End theatre ticket.

A night at the **opera** may mean watching the English National Opera (who sing all works in English) at the Coliseum in St. Martin's Lane, or the prestigious Royal Opera Company

Understanding Cricket

The quintessential English game is basically quite simple. There are two teams of eleven players, and both teams wear white. The two batsmen belong to one team, the bowler and ten fielders belong to the other team. It is their objective to remove the batsmen either by knocking the wicket down or catching the ball off the bat without it bouncing (once a batsman is "out" he is replaced by another member of his team, until all eleven players have batted). Meanwhile the batsmen score "runs" by galloping between the stumps. The team that scores the most runs wins the match.

The Royal Festival Hall forms part of a huge cultural complex on London's South Bank.

performing in the Royal Opera House in Covent Garden. This lovely stage is also home to the **Royal Ballet**. If advance bookings are sold out, one ticket per caller is on sale from 10:00 A.M. on the day of the performance, though be prepared for long queues. The Royal Ballets also play under the stars in mid-summer at the open-air theatre in Holland Park.

When it comes to **modern dance** you can't do better than the London Contemporary Dance Theatre, based at the Place Theatre (17 Duke's Road, WC1), or the Ballet Rambert, based at the capital's leading contemporary dance venue, Sadler's Wells Theatre in Islington (Rosebery Ave, EC1).

Classical **concerts** take place primarily at the South Bank Arts Centre, the Barbican, and the Royal Albert Hall. Smaller, more intimate venues include Wigmore Hall (Wigmore Street, off Oxford Street), St. John's Church, Smith Square (near Westminster Abbey) and St. Martin-in-the-Fields in Trafalgar Square. If you are in town between mid-July and mid-September, don't miss the informal Henry Wood Promenade Concerts (the "Proms") at the Royal Albert Hall. Holders of cheap tickets (on sale one hour beforehand) sit, stand, or even walk round (hence the name, from promenade) while the music plays. Pandemonium breaks out on the last night, when young lovers of classical music show their appreciation with football-crowd fervour.

Lunchtime concerts of chamber, organ or choral music are one of the great pleasures of everyday London culture. They usually start at 1:00 P.M. and venues include the two churches mentioned above plus many of Wren's delightful City churches. Performances are free, but do make a donation towards church maintenance. For details pick up a leaflet from the City Tourist Information Office at St. Paul's Churchyard.

Ever since the sixties, London has been the mecca for all forms of **rock and pop music**, with hundreds of bands playing in the city every week. You can nearly always catch major world acts playing in large, soulless arenas such as Wembley or Earl's Court, but smoky pubs and clubs are the real London scene. London is also home to some excellent jazz venues. Ronnie Scott's on Frith Street in Soho is the longest-established and best of the bunch, though Soho and Covent Garden in general boast a number of good jazz clubs and restaurants where the music is as important as the food.London's **nightclubs** are as vibrant and cosmopolitan as anywhere in the world. Some clubs have a different type of music—and crowd—every night, so read the listings magazines to make sure you know what you are going to! Dressing the part is the key to getting in: most clubs do not require membership, but bouncers will turn you away if you are too scruffy, or even too smart!

Cosmopolitan is also the term to describe London's **cinema** scene. The blockbusters play in the West End, particularly on Leicester Square, but look around and you can catch films from every era and every part of the world.

For weekly details of all London's entertainment look in the listings magazines published each Wednesday (*Time Out* or *What's On*).

Calendar of Events

January/February *Chinese New Year*. Traditional Lion dances around Soho's Chinatown.

March/April *Oxford versus Cambridge University Boat Race*. Eight oarsmen from each side slug it out up the Thames from Putney to Mortlake.

April *London Marathon*. The world's largest marathon with some 30,000 runners raising £5 million for various charities.

May *Chelsea Flower Show**. The most prestigious annual gardening exhibition in the world.

June *Beating the Retreat**. Marching bands acknowledge the "retreat" or setting of the sun in Horse Guards Parade.

Trooping the Colour*. The Queen inspects the troops at her official birthday parade (Saturday nearest 11 June).

All England Lawn Tennis Championships*. The world's greatest tennis players compete for the Wimbledon title.

July/September *Henry Wood Promenade Concerts**. Classical music made fun for eight weeks at the Royal Albert Hall.

August *Notting Hill Carnival*. The West Indian community bring a touch of Rio to London in Europe's largest street festival.

November *State Opening of Parliament*. Watch the Queen and Royal Procession en route to re-open Parliament after the summer recess.

Lord Mayor's Show. A popular pageant of carnival floats and the newly elected Lord Mayor in procession from the Guildhall to the Law Courts.

December *Christmas Tree and Carols in Trafalgar Square*. Choirs sing nightly beneath the giant tree, presented every year since 1947 by the people of Oslo.

*Spectating at these events is by ticket only. Enquire at tourist information offices well in advance of your trip.

EATING OUT

People who criticize English cooking are years out of date. There's a talented new generation of chefs in the kitchen and interest in traditional foods and methods of preparation is reviving. Moreover, many British people have had their palates educated by eating abroad on holidays so they now demand the same quality of food at home. Add to that the huge range of ethnic eating houses and you have a dynamic and evolving gastronomic city.

Where to Eat

If you just want a snack and you're on a limited budget then your best bet is probably a pub or wine bar. In some cases the latter are no more than restaurants with an extended wine list; the best kind, often to be found in the City, are dark and old-fashioned with sawdust on the floor, and are usually full of business types in pinstripes. The quality of pub food varies enormously, but as many establishments serve from a buffet at least you know what you are getting before ordering.

International Restaurants

There isn't a significant cuisine in the world that is not repre-sented in London. You can choose from Afghan to Viet-namese, with just about every shade of regional cooking in between. The top end is still dominated by the French, though home-grown chefs are making a determined assault with their own brand of cooking in which the best of British meets the best of international food. The style known as Modern British is a match for any cuisine in the world. Italian food has al-ways been very popular and a number of restaurants are now getting well away from the old-fashioned image of lashings of pasta and oversize pepper mills.

Indian and Chinese restaurants dominate the ethnic scene and these can be an excellent lunch time choice with bargain set-price buffets. Try dim sum (savoury dumplings) in any of Soho's Chinese restaurants during the day. The interest in Eastern food has grown so that Thai, Malaysian and latterly Vietnamese restaurants are becoming well established in London.

Hours

Cafes, wine bars and exotic restaurants add spice to Covent Garden's lively street culture.

In the more time-honoured establishments in London breakfast is usually served from around 8:00 A.M. or earlier to 10:30 A.M., and lunch is from noon to 2:30 P.M. Afternoon tea is served from 3:00 to 5:00 P.M. and dinner runs from 7:00 to 11:00 P.M. In practice you can eat what you want when you want if only you know where to look in London. The most comprehensive guide is the *Time Out Guide to Eating and Drinking in London*. If in doubt, Soho and Covent Garden are the best places for informal eating right round the clock.

With the liberalization of Britain's archaic licensing hours, many pubs now open all day from 11:00 A.M. to 11:00 P.M. Monday to Saturday. Sunday hours are noon to 3:00 P.M. and 7:00 to 10:30 P.M. If you want to drink later in a social atmosphere you will have to go to a club.

Breakfast

Start the day with a good old-fashioned full English breakfast of bacon, sausage, eggs, tomatoes, and perhaps mushrooms. At the better establishments kippers and, during the winter, porridge may be on the menu. If this sounds a little heavy, don't worry, as breakfast cereals and the Continental option of croissants and coffee are nearly always available.

Lunch

If you do choose a pub then it's always worth looking to see what the ploughman's lunch is like. This consists of bread, cheese (or ham, pâté, or sausage), salad, and pickle. If the bread is good and the cheese is a good wedge of tasty farmhouse Cheddar or Stilton (or the ham is fresh off the bone) then this can be delicious, but in many pubs, unfortunately, the standard is not high. If you cannot see what is on offer simply ask what on the menu is homemade. Scotch eggs are hard-boiled eggs wrapped in sausage meat and deep fried, and Cornish pasties (pronounced PAS-teas) are pastries filled with a mixture of beef and vegetables. They may sound tempting but invariably are pre-packed. You are more likely to get the home-made variety in the provinces.

Hot food in pubs may include baked/jacket potatoes, steak and kidney or chicken and mushroom pie, and shepherd's pie, a casserole of minced lamb (or beef, when it may be called cottage pie), carrots, and onions, topped with mashed potatoes.

Fish and chip shops serve cod, plaice, haddock, and sometimes rock salmon (a kind of dogfish), all battered and deep fried. Look for a place with a queue that is long!

If you want a real taste of the old East End look for a Pie & Mash Shop (most close on Sunday). The eponymous meal consists of minced beef pie and mashed potatoes with a strange green sauce made from parsley and called liquor (though not of the alcoholic variety). Eels are also on the menu. Not surprisingly, most of these are in the east of London. The nearest true Pie & Mash shop to the West End is Cookes at The Cut, by Waterloo Station.

Afternoon Tea

A grand old hotel or an exclusive department store is the place for that special afternoon tea. Order thinly sliced sandwiches (egg and cress, smoked salmon, cucumber, or tomato) scones, similar to American biscuits, but sweeter, or crumpets (like American-style English muffins), with jam. Or have a piece of fruit cake. A "cream tea" means scones with cream and jam. In the West Country you would be served clotted cream (a delicious thick, cooked cream) but in London you will probably get ordinary whipped cream. Traditional establishments may offer Welsh rarebit at tea time—melted cheese mixed with mustard and beer, spread on toast and browned under a grill. The tea itself may be an unspecified blend of Indian or China, smoky Lapsang Souchong, scented Earl Grey, Assam, Darjeeling, or any one of a dozen different types.

The George Inn, Southwark

This fine 17th-century pub, mentioned by Charles Dickens in *Little Dorrit* and probably also used by Dr. Johnson, is the only galleried inn left in London. When strolling actors, among them one William Shakespeare, appeared on the scene around the turn of the 17th century, inns added theatrical entertainment to their services. Performances took place in the courtyard while drinkers would watch from the galleries. In the summer, performances of the Bard's plays are still staged here. You will find the George Inn just off Borough High Street, 185 metres (200 yards) from London Bridge.

London's Pubs

The capital claims more than 5,000 public houses. The oldest date back nearly 500 years but even Victorian pubs seem laden with centuries of social history. Try the following for atmosphere, historical interest, good beer, and often good food.

The West End: The Grenadier, Old Barrack Yard, Wilton Row, Knightsbridge; Red Lion, Waverton Street, Mayfair; Red Lion, Duke of York Street, St. James's (closed on Sundays); The Albert, Victoria Street (between Victoria station and Parliament Square); The French House (an oddity, try the French wine, rather than the beer!), Dean Street, Soho; The Lamb, The Sun, both on Lamb's Conduit Street, WC1; The Lamb & Flag, Rose Street, Covent Garden.

The City: Ye Olde Cock Tavern, Fleet Street; Ye Olde Cheshire Cheese, Wine Office Court off Fleet Street; The Cittie of Yorke, High Holborn; The Blackfriar, Queen Victoria Street, by Blackfriar's Bridge; The Jamaica Wine House, St. Michael's Alley, Cornhill; The Cartoonist, Shoe Lane off Chancery Lane; Ye Olde Watling by St. Paul's. Note that most City pubs close at weekends.

By law, children under 14 cannot enter a pub; children over 14 must be accompanied by an adult and cannot purchase or drink alcohol. A 16-year-old may drink certain alcoholic drinks in the restaurant only, at the discretion of the landlord. The minimum age to be served alcohol is 18, though this too is at the landlord's discretion. If you have children with you it is worth seeking out pubs with gardens or family rooms (i.e., without a bar) where children are made welcome.

Dinner

Wherever possible, book in advance, especially for an after-theatre meal.

Starters

It may be hard to find British specialites in London's huge mix of restaurants but the following are traditional starters: smoked Scottish salmon or, in a fish restaurant, Colchester oysters; potted shrimps cooked with butter and spices and preserved in earthenware jars; country pâtés made from chicken or pork livers.

Main courses

The English answer to everything is a soothing cup ot tea.

England's classic dish is roast beef and crusty Yorkshire pudding. Roast leg of lamb is served with tangy mint sauce, while apple sauce is the usual accompaniment to roast pork. Roasts are normally served only on a Sunday in traditional English restaurants, hotels and, some pubs. At any other time the best place in London for roasts is Simpson's-in-the-Strand (see page 140).

Other traditional English dishes include hot pies (for instance steak and kidney) and game such as wild duck, pheasant, partridge, and venison. Salt beef is a delicious dish that you may find in the East End. The English enjoy their steak almost as much as their American counterparts but portions tend to be considerably smaller, and compared to other dishes is an expensive choice.

The best fish restaurants in the capital feature the freshest seafood: Dover sole, delicious grilled, or the somewhat less expensive and less delicately flavoured lemon sole; plaice, prepared simply with lemon and butter; turbot, with lobster and shrimp sauce; baked trout with bacon; poached or grilled fresh salmon, in mouthwatering steaks with Hollandaise sauce or made into fishcakes. Many seafood houses also serve oysters and the place to eat these in real style (and at great expense!) is at the Bibendum Oyster Bar, housed in the splendid 1930s Michelin building at 81, Fulham Road.

London's best fish restaurants feature the freshest seafood, immaculately prepared.

A side dish of vegetables usually comes with the main course. This is often, though not always, included in the price of the main dish—scrutinize the menu before ordering.

Desserts

Traditional English "sweets" or "puddings" range from a light fruit fool (puréed fruit mixed with cream), or a syllabub (includes wine) to a heavy, rib-sticking jam roly-poly or treacle pudding. These desserts may be suet-based, and flavoured with jam, treacle, or fruit, then steamed. Fruit pies and crumbles, with a top crust of crumbly pastry, are old favourites. Look out, too, for sherry trifle—fruit, jelly and sponge fingers soaked in sherry, and topped with set custard and whipped cream.

Cheese

Don't miss the opportunity to sample a selection of English cheeses: Stilton, a blue-veined cheese; Cheddar, which comes

in a number of varieties ranging from mild to sharp; Double Gloucester, a tangy orange-red cheese; Caerphilly from Wales, a mild white crumbly cheese; and Derby, mild and creamy, particularly good with fruit. Cheese is usually eaten with cheese biscuits (crackers) rather than bread.

In London pubs are an essential part of the city's social fabric.

Drinks

Sherry is the most genteel aperitif, followed by gin and tonic. Martini (vermouth) and Campari are also popular. If you ask for whisky you'll be served scotch unless you specify otherwise— Irish, Canadian and bourbon are usually available.

Beer is the traditional British drink, and when you ask for a beer in a pub you will be given the brown-coloured brew known as bitter. The "bitter" taste comes from the addition of hops to the brew but, despite its name, many bitters are quite sweet and fruity. You no longer have to ask for "real ale" (beer made and served in the traditional way) in London as almost every pub now serves it anyway. The chilled pale drink known to Americans and Europeans as beer is "lager" to the British. Pubs often serve many different types of beer so look at the dispensing pumps and specify the name of the beer you want to try. Or ask the bar staff for a "half" (a half pint) of their lowest-strength bitter then work your way up to the stronger brews! If you don't like bitter, don't worry. American and Continental lagers are almost as popular as the traditional British brew in London pubs these days.

INDEX

HANDY TRAVEL TIPS

An A–Z Summary of Practical Information

A

ACCOMMODATION see also CAMPING and YOUTH HOSTELS.

London's luxury hotels enjoy worldwide acclaim and the capital's medium–expensive range also meets international standards. At the budget end of the scale London is not so well served, though more bed and breakfast ("B&B") accommodation is becoming available.

Hotels and guesthouses are inspected and categorized according to the facilities they offer. The grades start at "listed" and go up from 1 through 5 crowns. However, this rating does not reflect the character of the establishment or the personal service that is offered there.

London's hotels are full much of the time so try to make arrangements well in advance. If you do arrive without anywhere to stay go to one of the London Tourist Information Centres (listed on pages 126). Here you can pick up various brochures including "Accommodation with Families in London," "Accommodation for Budget Travellers", and "Self-Catering Apartments and Accommodation Agencies in London." An on-the-spot booking service is also available for a charge of £5. You will be required to pay a deposit on the accommodation. Alternatively you can book by telephone (credit cards only) through London Tourist Board's Telephone Accommodation Booking Service; tel. 0171-824 8844. If you write to the London Tourist Board (LTB) at least six weeks in advance stating your budget and requirements, a reservation can also be made. Their address is: 26 Grosvenor Gardens, London SW1W 0DU. Uptown Reservations also runs a comprehensive bed and breakfast booking service, offering well-situated accommodation in private homes in central London; tel. 0171 351 3445.

Budget travellers can also book a hostel at central London tourist information offices at a reduced fee of £1.50 per person (maximum £4.50). If you are travelling throughout Britain you can "book a bed ahead" anywhere in the country, through the London offices .

London

AIRPORTS

London is principally served by two major airports, Heathrow (mostly scheduled flights) and Gatwick (scheduled and charter flights). Two smaller and more distant airports are Luton and Stansted.

Heathrow, one of the world's busiest airports, is located 24 km (15 miles) west of central London. The Piccadilly underground line (i.e. subway) provides the quickest (about 50 minutes) and cheapest link to all parts of London. However, if it is rush hour and you are laden wth luggage you may prefer to take a taxi (maximum 4/5 people) or catch the London Transport Airbus which goes to either Victoria or Euston train stations with several stops at popular hotels en route. Buses depart every 20–30 minutes and the journey time is usually around one hour.

Gatwick airport lies 43 km (27 miles) south of London. The British Rail (BR) Gatwick Express departs regularly for Victoria and takes around 30 minutes. Flightline 777 coaches make the journey in around 75 minutes.

B

BABYSITTERS

Most large hotels will provide a baby listening service and your hotel receptionist should also be able to help you with other child-minding arrangements. Childminders (tel. 0171-935 3000) is a reputable agency with over 25 years' experience. Expect to pay an initial registration fee of £5 then £11–14 for four hours plus travel expenses. Universal Aunts (tel. 0171-738 8937) is another good organization that provides a wide range of escort services for both young and old.

C

CAMPING

Write ahead to the London Tourist Board for the brochure "Camping Sites in and around London" (see TOURIST INFORMATION).

CAR HIRE see also DRIVING.

Heavy traffic and lack of parking space mean that a car is more of a hindrance than a help in central London. Public transport is quite adequate for trips to Windsor, Kew, and Hampton Court, so it is only advisable to hire a car if you want to explore farther afield. To do so you must be at least 21 years old and have held a driving licence for one year. Virtually all the world's driving licences are recognized.

CHILDREN see CHILDREN'S LONDON and BABYSITTERS.

If you do run out of ideas on how to keep little ones amused, call the London Tourist Board's "What's on for children" line for some friendly advice (tel. 0839-123424, calls charged at up to 49p per minute).

CLIMATE

London is fun to visit in any season, although in mid-winter it can be wet, windy, and cold. To cheer you up you'll find the world of entertainment in full swing and, of course, there are always the museums.

Temperatures	J	F	M	A	M	J	J	A	S	O	N	D
average daily F	43	44	50	56	62	69	71	71	65	58	50	45
maximum * C	6	7	10	13	17	20	22	22	19	14	10	7
average daily F	36	36	38	42	47	53	56	56	52	46	42	38
minimum *C	2	2	3	6	8	12	3	13	11	8	5	4

*Maximum temperatures are measured in the early afternoon, minimum temperatures before sunrise.

CLOTHING

London probably isn't as cold or as wet as you may have imagined, but do pack some light rainwear and something to keep off the evening chill, even in summer. In winter the wind may make you feel colder than the thermometer suggests. Even indoors you may need to wrap up as the British, great believers in fresh air (though rarely in air conditioning), do not overheat their homes.

The usual social convention is to dress as you please. Only a handful of conservative restaurants retain dress restrictions, and casual but chic attire is rarely out of place. Theatre-goers usually only dress up for premières or other special occasions.

COMMUNICATIONS

Post Offices:

Opening hours. Generally 9am–5:30 or 6pm Monday–Friday, 9am–12 or 12:30pm Saturdays. Provincial and suburban offices may close for lunch. The post office at 24–28 William IV Street (just off Trafalgar Square) is open 8am–8pm Monday–Saturday.

Poste Restante (General Delivery). If you don't know where you will be staying in London, you can have mail sent to you c/o poste restante. The most convenient office to specify may be William IV Street (see above). Take your passport or identity card when you go to pick up mail.

Stamps are sold at post office counters and from vending machines outside post offices. They are also now sold in a variety of other shops (newsagents etc.), often indicated by a red "stamps" sign.

Telephones:

The old familiar red boxes are now mostly gone, replaced by cubicles provided by British Telecom (BT) or Mercury. All include easy-to-understand instructions.

Coin-operated payphones take 10p, 20p, 50p, and £1 coins. Calls may be dialled direct anywhere in the world. Wholly unused coins will be returned at the end of the call so always feed in small coins if you can.

Phonecards can be bought from post offices or most newsagents in various denominations and eliminate the need for small change. You can make any number of calls to the value of the card by inserting it into the slot as instructed and taking it out when you have finished your call to use it again. Some BT and all Mercury phones also accept major credit cards.

Call charges. Mercury calls can be cheaper than BT (and as fewer people own Mercury cards so queues are shorter). Most calls (BT or Mercury) are cheaper in the evening: inland 6pm–8am, international 8pm–8am Beware hotel telephone surcharges.

   N.B. The prefix 0171 indicates that a number is within central London, 0181 is Greater London (though this may only be a few miles from the centre).

Telegrams. Telemessages have replaced inland (domestic) telegrams. Overseas telegrams and telemessages may be sent from any phone. Dial 190.

Useful numbers. Call the operator on 100 for general inland/domestic queries or if you are having difficulties getting through. For "Directory Enquiries" (if you are calling from within London) tel. 142; if you are calling from outside London, tel. 192. For International Directory Enquiries tel. 153; for international operator tel. 155.

COMPLAINTS

If your complaint is against a tourist attraction and you cannot resolve it directly with the manager, take your case to the nearest London Tourist Board Information Centre (see page 126).

   If you are unhappy with a purchase, which does not correspond to its description or is defective in some way, then as long as you can show some proof of purchase you have the right to return it. If the shop refuses this, or if you have any other problems involving overcharging or bad workmanship, consult a local Citizen's Advice Bureau (see the London *Yellow Pages* phone directory). The CAB's Greater London office, located at 136–144 City Road, EC1 (tel. 0171-251 2000), will also be able to provide local CAB numbers.

CRIME

While London's crime rate is lower than that of many American cities, it is rising. Be on your guard after dark away from crowded streets and in the underground. Watch out for pickpockets in crowded department stores, on public transport, and in street markets. Lock your car whenever you park it and remove any items of value.

In an emergency, dial 999 from any telephone (no money or card required). Otherwise phone the nearest police station, listed under "Police" in the telephone directory.

CUSTOMS and ENTRY FORMALITIES see also DRIVING.

Americans, South Africans, and citizens of EU countries need only a valid passport for tourist visits. However, travellers from some Commonwealth countries must have a visa. Check before departure. There are no passport controls between Britain and the Republic of Ireland.

Upon arrival you will have to fill in an entry card stating the address where you will be staying. The immigration officer will stamp your passport, allowing you to stay in Britain for a specific length of time. If your plans are uncertain ask for several months so you don't have to apply for an extension later. Provided you look respectable and have sufficient funds to cover your stay there should not be a problem.

In British ports and airports, passengers with goods to declare follow the red channel; those with nothing to declare take the green route.

The following chart shows which main duty-free items you may take into Britain and, when returning home, into your own country:

Into:	Cigarettes		Cigars	Tobacco	Spirits		Wine
Britain*	200	or	50	or 250 g	1 *l*	and	2 *l*
Australia	200	or	250 g	or 250 g	1 *l*	or	1 *l*
Canada	200	and	50	and 900 g	1.1 *l*	or	1.1 *l*
Eire	200	or	50	or 250 g	1 *l*	and	2 *l*
N Zealand	200	or	50	or 250 g	1.1 *l*	and	4.5 *l*
S Africa	400	and	50	and 250 g	1 *l*	and	2 *l*
USA	200	and	100	and **	1 *l*	or	1 *l*

* For non-European residents allowances also apply to non-duty free goods.

** a reasonable quantity

Currency restrictions: There is no limit on how much foreign currency you may import into Britain, and the export of pounds is not restricted. Check to see whether your own country has any regulations on the import and export of currency.

D

DRIVING see also CAR HIRE.

If you are bringing in your own car or one from Europe you will need the registration papers and insurance coverage. The usual formula is the Green Card, an extension to the normal insurance, validating it for other countries.

The driver and front-seat passenger must use seat belts; rear passengers must also use seat belts where they are fitted. Motorcycle and pillion riders must wear a crash helmet and a driving licence is required for all types of motorcycle. Sixteen is the lower age limit for mopeds, seventeen for motorcycles and scooters.

Driving conditions. Remember to drive on the left. Pay special attention at crossings (corners) and roundabouts (traffic circles). Traffic already on the roundabout has precedence over cars waiting and the rule is to give way to the right.

Driving through London is difficult even for the locals. If you must drive, study a good map in advance (preferably one that indicates which streets are one-way only) and note which local districts you will be heading through, as sometimes these are the only names signposted. It is also very helpful to have a good navigator!

Speed limits: In built-up areas 48 or 64 km/h (30 or 40 mph); on motorways (expressways) 112 km/h (70 mph); on other roads 80 or 96 km/h (50 or 60 mph).

Parking. Parking meters in central London are expensive at around £2 per hour, and the stay is often limited to two or four hours (cost and permitted duration indicated on meter). Don't be tempted to overstay or park where you shouldn't — a yellow line means no parking, a double yellow line means no waiting. Parking is particularly restricted between 8:30am–6:30pm Monday–Friday and 8:30am–1:30pm on Saturdays. After these times you may be able to park on metered spaces free of charge, but do check. Never park in those inviting meterless spaces marked for permit holders or residents only. If you do contravene any of these regulations you risk a hefty fine or, even worse, the dreaded wheel clamp. This means an even heavier fine (at least £68) plus a lot of inconvenience reclaiming your vehicle. Even worse, if your car is towed away it will cost you around £135 to get it back! For longer stays use a multi-storey car park or an outdoor car park. These too are expensive but are often your only choice.

Fuel and oil. Petrol (gasoline) is now sold almost everywhere in litres (only a few traditionalists retain the old gallon measure). Most places sell unleaded fuel. Service stations are abundant everywhere except in central London.

Traffic police. Although traffic police are helpful and tolerant towards foreigners you will get no sympathy in the case of blatant speeding or drink-driving offences (see below). Their vehicles are not always marked.

Drinking and driving. If you plan to drink more than half a pint of beer or a single measure of spirits you had better leave the car behind. Penalties are severe, involving loss of licence, heavy fines, and even prison sentences.

Repairs. Members of motoring associations affiliated to the Automobile Association (AA) or the Royal Automobile Club (RAC) can take advantage of their speedy efficient breakdown services.

AA: Haymarket House, Haymarket, London SW1Y 4TP; tel. (0345) 500600 (information), (0800) 887766 (breakdown service).

RAC: Travel Information Service; tel. (0345) 333-222; tel. (0800) 828282 (breakdown service).

Road signs. Britain has adopted the same basic system of pictographs in use throughout Europe. The *Highway Code* is the official booklet of road usage and signs, available at most bookshops. The following written signs may not be instantly comprehensible:

British	*American*
Carriageway	Roadway
Clearway	No parking by highway
Diversion	Detour
Dual carriageway	Divided highway
Give way	Yield
Level crossing	Railroad crossing
Motorway	Expressway
No overtaking	No passing
Roadworks	Men working
Roundabout	Traffic Circle

E

ELECTRIC CURRENT

The standard current in England is 240 volt, 50 cycle AC. You will need an adaptor (available from airport shops) for any appliance you bring from home, as well as a converter unless the appliance is equipped with one. Most hotels have special sockets for shavers that operate on 240 or 110 volts.

EMBASSIES and CONSULATES

All the following are in London and are open to the public Monday–Friday (visa section often open for only part of the day):

Australia: Australia House, Strand, WC2B 4LA; tel. 0171-379 4334 (hours 10am–4pm)

Canada: Tourist Information, 1 Grosvenor Square, W1; information (hours 10–12pm) tel. 0171-887 5107; High Commission, (hours 9am–3pm); tel. 0171-258 6600.

Eire: 17 Grosvenor Place, SW1X 7HR; tel. 0171-235 2171 (hours 9:30am–5pm Passport office: tel. 0171-245 9033

New Zealand: New Zealand House, Haymarket, SW1Y 4TQ; tel. 0171-930 8422 (hours: passport office 10am–noon, 2–4pm, general tourist enquiries: 9am–5pm)

South Africa: South Africa House, Trafalgar Square, WC2N 5DP; tel. 0171-451-7299 (hours 10am–noon, 2–4pm)

USA: 24 Grosvenor Square, W1A 1AE; tel. 0171-499 9000 (hours 8:30am–5:30pm)

Consult the London *Yellow Pages* phone directory for all other embassies, consulates, etc. (listed under Embassies).

EMERGENCIES

For police, fire brigade or ambulance dial 999 from any telephone (no money or card required) and tell the operator which service you require.

ETIQUETTE

The reserved attitude and famous stiff upper lip of the average English person generally conceal an easy-going, good-hearted nature. Locals usually enjoy talking to foreigners and often only their traditional reserve holds them back. Don't be afraid of breaking the ice — the subject of the weather is a good opener!

You may be addressed as Sir or Madam by a waiter, a clerk, a shop assistant or a police officer. But you must never return the courtesy; it might even be construed as sarcasm. On a first meeting use the formal address Mr or Mrs (Smith). You will probably soon be on first-name terms. Young people, of course, are much more relaxed and encounter few formal barriers.

GETTING TO LONDON

By Air
There are direct daily flights to Heathrow and Gatwick from airports all over the world.

From North America. There are direct flights from Atlanta, Boston, Chicago, Dallas/Fort Worth, Los Angeles, Montreal, New York, San Francisco, Toronto, and other cities.

From Australia and New Zealand. There are several weekly flights from Sydney, Melbourne, and Perth and from Auckland to London with stops en route.

By Sea
Ferries link Britain with many ports on the Continent. The two major lines are P&O and Sealink Stena Line, which operate several crossings between the major channel ports. The fastest crossing of the English Channel is aboard the Hoverspeed hovercraft, which makes the Dover–Calais and Dover–Boulogne trip in just 35 minutes. Fast trains link most of these ports to London. The principal port, Dover, is on the main British Rail Intercity network just over 90 minutes from London. The Channel Tunnel provides a direct rail link between Britain and mainland Europe. *Eurostar* operate regular, rapid services between London Waterloo and Paris Gare du Nord, Lille, or Brussels, with a travel time of around three hours (tel. 01233 617575), while *Le Shuttle* service provides transport for private cars from Folkestone in Kent to Calais in France (tel. 0999-353-535).

London

For those who prefer to travel transatlantic in style the *Queen Elizabeth 2* (QE2) makes about a dozen return trips a year from Southampton to New York between April and December.

By rail.

You can include Britain on a Eurailpass which allows unlimited travel on trains in 17 countries and on certain ferries (available only if you reside outside Europe and North Africa).

GUIDES and TOURS

Get off to the right start with an introductory panoramic tour of the city. London Coaches runs the Original London Sightseeing Tour offering 90 minutes of the best of the central area with live commentary in English or taped commentary in eight other major languages. Tours depart regularly from Baker Street (by Piccadilly Circus/Haymarket Underground Station), Speakers' Corner (by Marble Arch) and Victoria Underground Station. London Coaches' London Plus tours provide the capital's only hop-on, hop-off tourist bus service, which lets you get on and off at more than 30 different stops in the central area as often as you like; tel. 0171-828 6449 for more details. Enquire at tourist information offices about the many other tours that are available.

A dozen different companies organize walking tours of the city, talking generally about an area or a period in time, a historical theme, or a personality within an area — Legal London (around the Inns of Court), Roman London (around the City), Jack the Ripper (East End), Charles Dickens (Bloomsbury/Holborn), Coleridge (Highgate) are just a few examples. Some companies offer guided pub walks that are usually general area tours with some historic pubs thrown in. These are highly recommended as a way of meeting other people. *What's On* and *Time Out* list times and meeting places. Daytime tours last for about two hours, pub tours are longer. Recommended operators are The Original London Walks (tel. 0171-624 3978), Historical Walks of London (tel. 0181-668 4019), and Footsteps, which leads multilingual tours (tel. 0162-275 4451).

River boat trips generally feature some kind of commentary — often of the good-humoured, chirpy Cockney variety. There are regular departures from Westminster Pier and Charing Cross Pier down to Greenwich, tel. 0171 930 9033 or 0171-839 3572 for details. Three companies run enjoyable canal cruises between Little Venice (near the Warwick Avenue/Camden Town underground stations) and Camden Lock from Easter to October: Jason's Trip, tel. 0171-286 6752; Jenny Wren, tel. 0171-485 4433; the London Waterbus Company, tel. 0171-482 2550. The tourist board also has a River Trips Information Line, tel. 0839 123432.

For a really unusual tour try a flight over London aboard a 1930's biplane from Duxford, 80 km (48 miles) northeast of London. Bookings required at least 24 hours in advance, tel. 01255 424671.

L

LANGUAGE

You may not catch the quick, slick, Cockney of a London cabbie, particularly if he is using rhyming slang, but then neither does the average person born beyond the sound of Bow Bells. Transatlantic differences are numerous. Here is an excerpt of some more common words (see also DRIVING):

British	*American*
bill	check (restaurant)
bonnet	hood (of car)
boot	trunk (of car)
caravan	trailer
chemist	druggist
first floor	second floor
lay-by	roadside parking space
lorry	truck
off-licence	liquor store
nappy	diaper
pavement	sidewalk
queue	stand in line

British	American
return	round-trip (ticket)
single	one-way (ticket)
lift	elevator
tube or underground	subway

LOST PROPERTY

If you want to claim the loss of any item on your insurance policy you must report it to the police, who will issue you with a form. If the item was on a bus or on the underground go to the London Transport Lost Property Office at 200 Baker Street, NW1 5RW (no telephone enquiries), open 9:30am–2pm Monday–Friday. Wait for two days after you lost the item before you call.

If you lost it in a train, contact the railway terminal to which you were heading. If you were in a black taxi, contact the Metropolitan Polic Lost Property Office, 15, Penton Street, N1 9PU; tel. 0171-833 0996.

M

MEDIA

Most newsstands carry copies of the *International Herald Tribune*, and American magazines are also widely available. However, while newspapers from Europe and the Middle East are easily obtained, periodicals from further afield in the English-speaking world are rare. Try your High Commission or national airline office if you are hungry for news from home.

To find out what's happening in London in the fields of arts, entertainment, sports, and nightlife it's a good idea to buy one of the weekly listings magazines — *What's On* or *Time Out*. *Time Out* is the most comprehensive and most Londoners' favourite, while *What's On* is strictly for tourists. Both of these come out on a Wednesday. The daily London *Evening Standard* is also a good source of information.

Standard television receivers pick up two BBC channels and two independent channels. Satellite dishes or special cables are needed to pick up other stations.

On the radio there are five BBC stations: pop music (Radio 1) 93.6–99.8 FM; easy listening (Radio 2) 89.1 FM; classical music and plays (Radio 3) 91.3 FM; news, current affairs and plays (Radio 4) 92.4–94.6 FM; sport, easy listening and chat (Radio 5) 909 MW. Listen to BBC local radio's GLR (Greater London Radio) on 94.9 FM for rock music, chat and what's on in town. There are several other commercial stations in the London area.

The BBC World Service (648 KHz/463 m) provides the most comprehensive international news coverage. If you are yearning to hear a voice from home you can pick up the Voice of America or Radio Canada International on a short-wave receiver. Check daily newspapers or listings magazines for full radio and TV coverage.

MEDICAL CARE

Britain enjoys high standards of public hygiene, medicine, and welfare, which should ensure a healthy holiday. Restaurants are regularly inspected and you can drink the tap water with confidence anywhere.

Although the National Health Service takes care of anyone in need of urgent attention free of charge, visitors from countries outside the EU have to pay for non-emergency treatment. Medical insurance is therefore strongly recommended. Your travel agent will be able to help you with a modestly priced policy. If you are taken ill you must first see a general practitioner (GP), whose task it is to diagnose and treat or, if necessary, to direct you to a specialist or hospital.

In case of emergency only, dial 999 for an ambulance. If you are ill outside normal consulting hours but your situation is not an emergency, there are 24-hour walk-in casualty departments at the following central London hospitals:

St. Thomas's, Lambeth Palace Road; tel. 0171-928 9292.

University College, Gower Street (entrance on Grafton Way); tel. 0171-387 9300.

London

Chelsea and Westminster, 369 Fulham Road, SW1; tel. 0181-746 8000.

Eye casualties should go to Moorfields Eye Hospital, City Road; tel. 0171-253 3411.

Chemists: Also referred to as pharmacies (rarely drugstores). Late-night-opening chemists include: Bliss, 5 Marble Arch, 9am–midnight, daily, tel. 0171-723 6116; Boots, 44–46 Regent Street, 8:30 am–8pm Monday–Friday, 9am–6pm Saturday, noon–6pm Sunday, tel. 0171-734 6126; Boots, 75 Queensway, 9am–10pm Monday–Saturday, tel. 0171-229 9266.

MONEY MATTERS

Currency. The monetary unit is the pound sterling (£), divided into 100 pence (p).

Banknotes: £5, £10, £20, £50

Coins: 1p, 2p, 5p, 10p, 20p, 50p, £1

For currency restrictions see CUSTOMS AND ENTRY FORMALITIES.

Banks and Currency Exchange Offices. The leading banks have "High Street branches" in all major shopping streets in London, including the suburbs. Many neighbourhood banks will be able to change your foreign currency or traveller's cheques (look for the "Foreign Exchange" sign). Private currency exchange offices are known as Bureaux de Change.

If you are exchanging a reasonable amount of money, shop around. Rates can vary considerably and bureaux de change in particular charge heavily for their handy locations and the convenience of late opening. If you do use one of these, make sure they are displaying an LVCB sticker or plaque.

Credit Cards and Traveller's Cheques. Credit cards are widely accepted in hotels, restaurants, and shops, but traveller's cheques are not. Change them in a bank or a bureau de change (same rules as for cash, see above). You will need your passport as proof of identity. Don't offer foreign currency as payment; the few establishments who do accept it will penalize you on the exchange rate.

Tax Refunds for Tourists. A sales tax called Value Added Tax (VAT), currently 17.5 percent, is levied on most shop goods in Britain. VAT is always included in the price displayed in store. Most big shops that have significant tourist trade participate in a scheme whereby non-EU travellers are refunded the VAT paid on goods less a small service charge. Participating shops usually display a "tax-free shopping" sticker. Your refund will be worth around 11 percent of the price you paid, so it is worth asking for. There is usually a minimum purchase price of £100 upwards and you must leave the country within three months to qualify. Ask the shop to issue you with the appropriate form (you may need your passport or other form of identification). This should be presented with the goods for validation to the customs officer at the airport or seaport of departure. A separate form is issued for larger goods that have to go into the cargo hold. The method of refund so far has been by cheque to the home address, but trials are in place at Heathrow whereby a cash refund is given to you as you depart.

For further information on VAT refunds contact the Shopping Advisory Service in the British Travel Centre on Regent Street.

PLANNING YOUR BUDGET

To give you an idea what to expect here are some average prices in pounds sterling (£). However annual inflation and other factors can cause sudden changes, so they must be regarded as approximate.

Airport transfers. Heathrow to Central London: taxi £34; underground (subway) to Piccadilly Circus £3.20; Airbus to Victoria or Euston via major hotels £6. Gatwick to London: taxi around £65; train to Victoria £8.90; Flightline 777 or 778 to Victoria £7.50.

Bus. Minimum 80p, average £1.30–2.30.

Car Hire (international company, unlimited mileage, tax and comprehensive insurance). Group A, £45 per day, £248 per week; Group B £55 per day, £283 per week; Group C £61 per day, £295 per week.

Entertainment. Cinema around £6; discotheque/club £8–10.

Guides. Walking tours £4.

Hotels (Central London, double room with bath, excluding breakfast, including VAT per night). ***** over £200; **** £160, *** £90; ** £70.

Meals and drinks. English breakfast £3 plus; Continental breakfast £2 plus; lunch (in pub including one drink) £6, dinner (three courses, including wine, reasonable restaurant) £25 plus; bottle house wine £7–8; pint of beer £1.80; whisky £1.50; soft drink £1; tea 60p–£1 per pot per person; coffee 60p–£1 per cup.

Museums and Art Galleries. £3–9 per adult; children usually half-price; family ticket often available (usually equivalent to second child free).

Tours. Bus tours central London £8; £10 with hop-on, hop-off facility.

Taxis (see also TAXIS, page 138). Meter starts automatically at £1.40, which is the minimum charge for the first 873 yards or 3 minutes. (An additional £2.80 is charged if the taxi has been booked by phone.) The fare is then 84p per km (£1.40 per mile) thereafter. Surcharges are as follows: 40p per additional passenger; 10p per piece of luggage stored next to the driver; 40p 8pm–midnight Monday–Friday and 6am–8pm Saturday; 60p midnight–6am Monday–Friday and 8pm Saturday–6am Monday as well as all public holidays.

Underground. Single central zone £1.10; all zones £3.20; one-day Travelcard (after 9:30am) two central zones £3.80; one-day LT card (any time) two central zones £3.90. Children £1.60 all zones.

OPENING HOURS

Banks: minimum hours 9:30am–3:30pm Monday–Friday. Some banks open for limited services on Saturday mornings.

Museums: 10am–5 or 6pm Monday–Saturday, and from 2 or 2:30–5 or 6pm on Sundays. Some museums open earlier on Sundays.

Offices: 9 or 9:30am–5 or 5:30pm Monday–Friday.

Pubs: Traditional hours 11am–3pm and 5:30–11pm Monday–Saturday, noon–2pm and 7–10:30pm Sundays. Extended hours 11am–11pm Monday–Saturday, noon–3pm and 7–10:30pm Sundays.

Shops: 9 or 9:30am–5:30 or 6pm Monday–Saturday. Covent Garden 10am–8pm Monday–Saturday and Sunday afternoon. Late-night shopping Wednesday till 7pm in Chelsea and Knightsbridge; Thursday till 7:30 or 8pm in Oxford and Regent Streets.

PHOTOGRAPHY and VIDEO

All leading makes and sizes of films are sold at photographic shops, chemists (drugstores), department stores and some supermarkets and souvenir shops. There are plenty of one-hour and 24-hour outfits in the central area where you can have your film developed. Chemists also accept film for developing and may be cheaper and better quality if you can wait for four or five days. All types of blank video tape are available, but note that pre-recorded cassettes sold here may not be compatible with the system at home.

POLICE

London police are unarmed and, on the whole, they are friendly and helpful. Do not expect leniency if you break the law, however. In case of emergency telephone 999.

PUBLIC HOLIDAYS

These are also known as bank holidays. Banks and offices are shut, but most forms of entertainment are open, on New Year's Day, Good Friday, Easter Monday, May Day (first Monday in May), Spring Bank Holiday (last Monday in May), Summer Bank Holiday (last Monday in August), Christmas Day (25 December and Boxing Day (26 December). If any of these holidays falls on a weekend, it is taken on the following Monday.

PUBLIC TRANSPORT

Buses. There is a frequent service of red doubledecker buses on an extremely dense and complicated network. You do sit in traffic jams, but at least you can see the sights and perhaps meet the locals. There are two types of bus sign: a red symbol on a white background indicates a compulsory stop (unless the bus is full); a white symbol on a red background indicates a request stop where you have to hold your arm out in plenty of time to let the driver know to stop. You will also have to ring the bell in advance of your stop to let the driver know you want to get off. If your bus is the old-fashioned type with an open rear platform just climb aboard and the conductor will come around and collect your fare en route. On other buses you may have to pay the driver as you board, so always have some change handy to avoid delay.

Express mini-buses also ply some of the popular routes and single-decker Green Line buses serve the suburbs and outskirts.

Most buses run from about 6am–11 or 11:30pm Night buses then take over running an hourly skeleton service. Many pass through Trafalgar Square so head there to be sure of catching one.

There are various types of travel card that allow unlimited travel on bus, underground and British Rail lines for various time periods. The London Visitor Travelcard is available only outside

Britain through British Rail offices and travel agents, and offers more or less unlimited travel for three, four or seven days. It comes with discount vouchers for a number of attractions, such as Madame Tussaud's. (See **Travel Information Centres** below).

Underground. The "tube," though initially daunting, is quite easy to get to grips with and is much the quickest way of travelling around London. Maps in the stations and on the trains show the various lines colour-coded for easy reference. Buy your ticket in the station entrance hall. On your way to the platform you will have to insert it into an automatic turnstile device which opens to let you through and returns your ticket — don't forget to take it back! You will not need to show it again (unless an inspector boards) until you leave the station at your destination.

Trains run from around 5:30am–midnight, Monday–Saturday, and from around 7am–11pm on Sundays. Smoking is strictly prohibited on any part of the underground.

Travel Information Centres. Free route maps and general information covering buses and the underground are available from Travel Information Centres at the following underground stations: Euston (BR concourse), Heathrow (station for terminals 1,2,3), King's Cross, Liverpool Street, Oxford Circus, Piccadilly Circus, St. James's Park, Victoria (BR concourse, opposite platform 8). There are also centres at all Heathrow air terminals in the arrivals area and at the British Travel Centre, Regent Street. Finally there is a telephone travel information service; tel. 0171-222 1234.

Trains. The principle mainline (as opposed to underground) stations are Euston, King's Cross, Liverpool Street, Paddington, St. Pancras, Victoria, and Waterloo. They are all connected to the underground.

Several discount passes for train travel are available. If you intend travelling around the country, consider the BritRail Pass, which allows unlimited travel for certain periods (sold outside Britain only). Ask at any mainline station for more information.

Docklands Light Railway (DLR). If you want a glimpse of the future, hop on to one of the DLR's fully automated, driverless trains for a trip to Docklands. The service starts underground at Bank or above ground at Tower Gateway (adjacent to Tower Hill underground station) and runs east quietly and smoothly on an elevated track past massive building works going on in the Docklands area, including Europe's tallest building, the 244-metre (800-foot) Canary Wharf Tower. Take the line to Island Gardens for the best views. You can get off here and walk under the Thames foot tunnel to Greenwich. Docklands is not yet a developed tourist area but there are information centres at Tower Gateway and Island Gardens. Trains run Monday–Friday 5:30am–12:30am For more information on the DLR; tel. 0171-538-9400.

R

RESTAURANTS see also Eating Out (pages 91-98) and Recommended Restaurants (pages 138-143).

London's restaurant scene is truly international and there are few, if any, general rules that apply to all restaurants. There is no official grading system but there are plenty of specialist guide books to advise you. The most critical are *The Good Food Guide* (published by the Consumer's Association) and the *Egon Ronay Guide*, although both of these cover the whole of Britain. The most comprehensive London restaurant guide is the *Time Out Guide to Eating and Drinking in London*, covering over 1,700 establishments from the humblest café to the Savoy Hotel.

Restaurant Switchboard is a free advisory service to which many London restaurateurs subscribe, although the advice they give is claimed to be impartial. If you're stuck for an idea they will be pleased to help out and will also book you a table free of charge; tel. 0181-888 8080.

RELIGION

The Church of England is the country's official church but freedom of religion is guaranteed. Virtually every major religious group in the world — including Jewish, Muslim, and Buddhist — has a place of worship in London. Many hotels display listings of nearby churches and times of services. The Saturday editions of the more heavyweight papers usually give information on the most prominent services.

 T

TAXIS

London's black cabs (which can also be white, green, red, or blue!) are rated the best in the world. They are spacious inside, mechanically superb, and to be licensed their drivers have passed extremely rigorous memory tests, including learning by heart over 620 well-worn routes within a 9.6 km (6-mile) radius of Charing Cross!

A taxi can be hailed on the street whenever its For Hire light is on. As long as the journey is under 6 miles (9.6 km) and wholly within the Metropolitan Police District the driver is obliged to take you and the fare payable is shown on the meter (see PLANNING YOUR BUDGET). Outside these restrictions the fare is negotiable and should be agreed beforehand. The exceptions are the airport routes, London–Heathrow, and London–Gatwick, which are metered.

Black cabs can be ordered by telephone 24 hours a day (note that you will be charged for being picked up as well as driven to your destination); tel. 0171-286 0286; 0171-272 0272; 0171-253 5000.

Other taxis operating in London are known as minicabs. Minicab drivers need no special qualifications and cars are generally not metered. By law they cannot be hailed in the street nor can they solicit trade. Never accept a lift from minicab drivers offering their services at the airport or station. If you want the number of a reputable local company your hotel should be able to help you.

A tip of 10 per cent is customary.

TIME DIFFERENCES

In winter Great Britain is on Greenwich Mean Time. In summer (April–October) clocks are put forward one hour.

London

Summer time differences:

New York	**London**	Jo'burg	Sydney	Auckland
7 am	**noon**	1 pm	9 pm	11 pm

TIPPING

Restaurants may add a service charge to your bill in which case the tip is included. If you do not feel the service warranted the charge you may deduct part or all of it, though you will have to justify this. Cinema and theatre ushers do not expect tips, nor do barstaff — though you may offer to buy them a drink. Never feel obliged to tip if the service has been no more than adequate. British people are far less aggressive about tipping than Americans. The chart below gives guidelines.

Hairdresser/barber	10–15%
Hotel maid per week	£3–4
Hotel porter per bag	50p
Taxi driver	10–15% (50p minimum)
Tourist Guide	10–15% (£1 minimum)
Waiter	10–15% (if service not included)

TOILETS

These may be marked in railway stations, parks and museums, as "Public Conveniences" or "WC" (water closet). If you are asking for directions, simply ask for the toilets. Remember that in Britain a bathroom is for bathing in, washing up means washing the dishes, and restroom means nothing at all!

TOURIST INFORMATION OFFICES

The British Tourist Authority will provide you with information before you leave home:

Australia: 210 Clarence Street, Sydney, New South Wales 2000; tel. (2) 267-4442

Canada: Suite 600, 111 Avenue Road, Suite 450, Toronto, Ontario M5R 3J8; tel. (416) 925-6326

South Africa: Lancaster Gate, Hyde Park Lane, Hyde Park, Sandton 2196; tel (11) 325-0343

USA: Suite 1510, 625 North Michigan Avenue, Chicago, IL 60611; tel. (312) 787-0490

Suite 450, World Trade Center, 350 South Figueroa Street, Los Angeles, CA 900171; tel. (213)-628-3525

551 Fifth Avenue, New York, New York 10176-0799; tel. (212) 986-2200, (toll free) 1-800-GO-2-BRITAIN.

The London Tourist Board and Convention Bureau is the official body concerned with tourism in London. Write for information to: 26 Grosvenor Gardens, London SW1W 0DU.

The central tourist information offices are at Victoria Station forecourt; Selfridges, Oxford Street (basement); Liverpool Street underground station; Heathrow Terminals 1,2,3 underground station. All are open daily. The British Travel Centre, 12 Regent Street, deals with all areas of Britain and is useful for sorting out travel arrangements. For information on the City of London consult the tourist information centre at St. Paul's Churchyard, in the shadow of the cathedral; tel. 0171-332 1456.

The London Tourist Board telephone information service gives information on London; tel. 0839-123456; dial the following last three digits for specific information (all are preceded by 0839-123): 400 what's on this week; 403 current exhibitions; 411 Changing of the Guard; 416 popular West End shows; 424 where to take the children; 480 Popular attractions; 481 palaces; 429 museums; 431 tours and walks; 432 river cruises.

TRAVELLERS with DISABILITIES

Many museums, theatres and restaurants provide access and facilities for the disabled traveller but it is always advisable to telephone ahead to request assistance and ascertain any particular requirements. The definitive guide book is Nicholson's *Access in London*, available in some bookshops (all good bookshops will order you a copy, quote ISBN 0-9485-7638-3). The LTB also provides a free leaflet, "London For All," available from Information Centres. Artsline is a free telephone information service for disabled people in London, covering the arts and entertainments; tel. 0171-388 2227 9:30am–5:30pm Monday–Friday.

For details on public transport pick up "Access to the Underground," free from Tourist Information Centres or by post from London Regional Transport, Unit for Disabled Passengers, 55 Broadway, London SW1; tel. 0171-918 3312.

The Holiday Care Service produces a brochure "Accessible Accommodation in London," available from Tourist Information Centres or from Holiday Care Service, 2 Old Bank Chambers, Station Road, Horley, Surrey RH6 9HW; tel. (01293) 774535.

William Forrester is a wheelchair user who in 1989 became the first-ever winner of the London Tourist Board's award for the best London Guide of the year. His tours are always informative and highly entertaining; tel. (01483) 575401 as far ahead as possible.

Y

YOUTH HOSTELS see also ACCOMMODATION.

There are seven youth hostels in central London including interesting accommodation in the old St. Paul's choir school building in the City and a Jacobean mansion in Holland Park. Other locations are Earl's Court, Highgate, Hampstead, Oxford Street and Rotherhithe (Docklands). You must be a member to stay in one of these but joining is inexpensive and so are room rates which are around £9–11 per night including breakfast. You will have to book two or three months in advance; tel. (0171) 248 6547 for details.

There are also 18 YMCA hotels around London, which offer slightly more expensive accommodation. Contact the National Council for YMCAs; tel. 0181-520 5599.

Recommended Hotels

Choosing a hotel in a city that you're not familiar with can be daunting. In London there are hotel booking facilities at the main tourist information offices (see ACCOMMODATION, page 103 and TOURIST INFORMATION, page 126). In this section we list some tried and trusted hotels to get you started.

The telephone area code for a particular section of London is given after the regional headings. The symbols below are a guide to the price of a standard double room with bathroom. Breakfast is usually extra. Where B&B (bed and breakfast) is stated the price includes accommodation and breakfast. All prices are inclusive of service and tax.

✪	Budget (below £50)
✪✪	Moderate (£50–£100)
✪✪✪	Expensive (£100–£180)
✪✪✪✪	Luxury (above £180)

BAYSWATER (0171)

London Embassy ✪✪✪ *150 Bayswater Road, W2 4RT; tel. 229 1212; fax 229 2623.* Stylish modern establishment with good facilities and standards of comfort. Views over Kensington Gardens. 193 rooms.

Mornington (B&B) ✪✪ *12 Lancaster Gate, W2 3LG; tel. 262 7361, fax 706 1028.* Bed and breakfast in a Victorian town house with a homely atmosphere. Good value for money. 68 rooms.

BLOOMSBURY (0171)

Academy ✪✪-✪✪✪ *17–21 Gower Street, WC1E 6HG; tel. 631 4115 800-678-3096, fax 636 3442.* Elegant Georgian terraced house with high standards of service and comfort. 36 rooms.

Bedford ✪✪ *83 Southampton Row, WC1 B3LB; tel. 636 7822.* Refurbished hotel with good facilities and a lovely little garden. Situated near the City and the British Museum. Breakfast included. 184 rooms.

Kenilworth ✪✪✪ *97 Great Russell Street, WC1 B3LB; tel. 637 3477, fax 631 3133.* Elegant Edwardian-style hotel in a quiet backwater; romantic restaurant. 192 rooms.

Russell ✪✪✪ *Russell Square, WC1 N1LN; tel. 837 6470, fax 837 2857.* Beautiful Victorian building on the lovely Russell Square. Traditionally furnished bedrooms. 326 rooms.

Whitehall ✪✪ *2–5 Montague Street, WC1 B5BP; tel. 580 5871, fax 323 0409.* Cosy, traditional Georgian terraced house just off Russell Square. 74 rooms.

CHARING CROSS (0171)

Royal Horse Guards Thistle Hotel ✪✪✪ *2 Whitehall Court, SW1 A2EJ; tel. 839 3400, fax 925 2263.* Large, cosy hotel in the buildings of the old National Liberal Club. Views of the Royal Festival Hall. 376 rooms.

CHELSEA (0171)

Cadogan ✪✪✪ *75 Sloane Street, SW1 X9SG; tel. 235 7141, fax 245 0994.* Delightful old hotel with its own garden and tennis court. Once the home of English actress Lillie Langtry. 71 rooms.

Magnolia Hotel (B&B) ✪-✪ *105 Oakley Street, SW3 5NT; tel. 352 0187.* Bed and breakfast accommodation in a pleasant Victorian terraced house just off fashionable King's Road. Good value. 24 rooms.

Wilbraham ✪✪ *1–5 Wilbraham Place, SW1 X9AE; tel. 730 8296, fax 730 6815.* Imaginatively and elegantly decorated hotel occupying three Victorian houses. 64 rooms.

Willett ✪✪ *32 Sloane Gardens, Sloane Square, SW1 W8DJ; tel. 824 8415, fax 730 4830.* Large, airy, well-equipped bedrooms in a smart Chelsea town house. 18 rooms.

COVENT GARDEN (0171)

Fielding ✪✪-✪✪✪ *4 Broad Court, Bow Street, WC2B 5Q2; tel. 836 8305, fax 497 0064.* A small, comfortable, friendly hotel which retains much of its 18th-century character. 26 rooms and 2 suites.

Pastoria ✪✪-✪✪✪ *36 St. Martin's Street, WC2H 7HL; tel. 930 8641, fax 925 0551.* Originally a gentleman's club, superbly renovated in thirties style. A stone's throw from the National Gallery. 58 rooms.

Savoy ✪✪✪✪ *The Strand, WC2R OEU; tel. 836 4343, fax 240 6040.* A hotel for the rich and famous, the Savoy is a London legend with a truly fascinating history. The Savoy Hotel Grill Room is first-rate, serving classic French and English cuisine. 202 rooms.

Waldorf ✪✪✪✪ *Aldwych, WC2B 4DD; tel. 836 2400, fax 836 7244.* Luxury Edwardian establishment opened in 1908 and completely refurbished in 1992. Afternoon tea dancing in the hotel's Palm Court. 292 rooms.

KENSINGTON & HOLLAND PARK (0171)

Atlas ✪ *24–30 Lexham Gardens, W8 5JE; tel. 835-1155, fax 370-4853.* Comfortable, reasonably priced hotel situated in a quiet residential area. 9 rooms.

Demetriou Guest House (B&B) ✪ *9 Strathmore Gardens, W8; tel. 229 6709.* Reasonably priced accommodation in an expensive area. Quiet cul-de-sac location. 9 rooms.

Halcyon ✪✪✪✪ *81 Holland Park, W11 3R2; tel. 727 7288, fax 229 8516.* Tastefully decorated rooms in an attractive Victorian town house with country-house atmosphere and antique furnishings. Friendly, courteous staff. 43 rooms.

Kensington Close ✪✪-✪✪✪ *Wright's Lane, W8 5SP; tel. 937 8170, fax 937 8289.* Modern hotel with gym, indoor pool, sauna, sunbeds, squash courts and water garden. Good value. 543 rooms.

KNIGHTSBRIDGE & BELGRAVIA (0171)

Basil Street ✪✪✪ *8 Basil Street, SW 1AH; tel. 581 3311, fax 581 3693.* Wonderfully old-fashioned hotel full of character and charm. Excellent restaurant. 93 rooms.

Beaufort ✪✪✪✪ *33 Beaufort Gardens, SW3 1PP; tel. 584 5252, fax 589 2834.* Charming, homely little hotel situated in a quiet square near Harrod's. 28 rooms.

Capital ✪✪✪-✪✪✪✪ *22–4 Basil Street, SW3 1AT; tel. 589 5171, fax 225 0011.* Small, quiet, beautifully decor-ated hotel with one of London's best restaurants. 48 rooms.

Claverly (B&B) ✪✪-✪✪✪ *13–14 Beaufort Gardens, SW3 1PS; tel. 589 8541, fax 584 3410.* Beautifully decorated, award-winning hotel. 31 rooms.

Hyde Park ✪✪✪✪ *66 Knightsbridge, SW1Y 7LA; tel. 235 2000, fax 235 7022.* Grand old Edwardian hotel overlooking Hyde Park. Rooms recently redecorated, many with antique furnishings. 130 rooms.

Lowndes ✪✪✪-✪✪✪ *21 Lowndes Street, SW1X 9ES; tel. 823 1234, fax 235 1154.* Small, quiet, charming hotel in an excellent location near Belgrave Square. 78 rooms.

MARYLEBONE & REGENT'S PARK (0171)

Colonnade ✪✪ *2 Warrington Crescent, W9 1ER; tel. 286 1052, fax 286 1057.* Two converted Victorian houses boasting an excellent standard of accommodation; good breakfasts and pleasant patio area. 49 rooms.

Dorset Square Hotel ✪✪✪ *39–40 Dorset Square, NW1 6QN; tel. 723 7874, fax 724 3328.* Elegant town-house hotel on Dorset Square, with English country-house atmosphere and antique furnishings. 37 rooms.

White House ✪✪✪ *Albany Street, NW1 3UP; tel. 387 1200, fax 388 0091, Res. tel. 388 8493.* Modern, airy and well-equipped rooms near Regent's Park. Excellent restaurant. Some weekend discounts. 600 rooms.

Brown's ✪✪✪✪ *29–34 Albermarle Street, W1A 45W; tel. 493 6020 or 800 225 5843, fax 493 9381.* Small, traditional hotel, famous for its afternoon tea. First-class service and comfort. 120 rooms.

Claridge's ✪✪✪✪ *Brook Street, W1A 2JQ; tel. 629 8860, fax 499 2210.* The ultimate in luxury and discreet service, popular with royals from all over the world. 189 rooms.

Connaught ✪✪✪✪ *16 Carlos Place, W1Y 6AL; tel. 499 7070 or 800 637 2869, fax 495 3262.* Splendidly decorated rooms, faultless service and one of London's top restaurants. 90 rooms.

London

Dukes ✪✪✪-✪✪✪✪ *35 St. James's Place, SW1A 1NY; tel. 491 4840, fax 493 1264.* Small, elegant Edwardian hotel tucked away in a gas-lit courtyard. 64 rooms.

London Hilton on Park Lane ✪✪✪✪ *22 Park Lane, W1Y 4BE; tel. 493 8000, fax 2084142.* Luxury high-rise hotel overlooking Hyde Park. 446 rooms, 53 suites.

Park Lane ✪✪✪✪ *Piccadilly, W1 Y8BX; tel. 499 6321, fax 499 1965.* Fine old twenties-style hotel, extensively renovated, overlooking Green Park. 350 rooms.

Ritz ✪✪✪✪ *150 Piccadilly, W1V 9DG; tel. 493 8181, fax 493 2687.* A byword for style and elegance, with beautiful public rooms. Afternoon tea in The Palm Court is a must. 131 rooms.

NOTTING HILL GATE (0171)

Holland Park (B&B) ✪✪ *6 Ladbrooke Terrace, W11; tel. 792 0216, fax 727 8166.* Beautifully restored Victorian town house. 23 rooms.

Pembridge Court ✪✪-✪✪✪ *34 Pembridge Gardens, W2 4DX; tel. 229 9977 or 800 709 9882, fax 727 4982.* Small 19th-century town house in quiet garden square. Price includes breakfast. 20 rooms.

Portobello ✪✪✪-✪✪✪✪ *22 Stanley Gardens, W11 2NG; tel. 727 2777, fax 792 9641.* Charming six-storey terraced house. 24-hour restaurant. Price includes breakfast. 25 rooms.

OXFORD STREET & BAKER STREET (0171)

Bickenhall ✪-✪✪ *119 Gloucester Place, W1H 3PJ; tel. 935 3401, fax 224 0614.* Elegant Georgian house with a pleasant patio area. Price includes breakfast. 23 rooms.

Concorde Hotel ✪✪ *50 Great Cumberland Place, W1 H7FD; tel. 402 6169, fax 724 1184.* Small, pleasant hotel, comfortably furnished. 28 rooms.

Durrant's ✪✪-✪✪✪ *26–32 George Street, W1H 6BJ; tel. 935 8131, fax 487 3510.* Old Georgian house with a dignified but cosy atmosphere. 96 individually designed rooms.

St. George's ✪✪ *Langham Place, W1N 8QS; tel. 580 0111, fax 436 7997.* Modern hotel, all rooms with panoramic views. Price includes breakfast. 86 rooms.

Savoy Court ✪✪ *Granville Place, W1H 0EH; tel. 408 0130, fax 493 2070.* Comfortably furnished Edwardian-style hotel hidden in a quiet mews. 100 rooms.

SOUTH KENSINGTON (0171)

Cranley Gardens ✪✪-✪✪✪ *8 Cranley Gardens, SW7 3DB; tel. 373-3232, fax 373 7944.* Pleasant hotel occupying four adjoining town houses, decorated in typical cosy English style. Friendly staff.

Gore ✪✪✪-✪✪✪✪ *189 Queen's Gate, SW7 5EX; tel. 584 6601, fax 589 8127.* Pleasant, quiet, small hotel with attractive decor. 53 rooms.

John Howard ✪✪ *4 Queen's Gate, SW7 5EH; tel. 581 3011, fax 589 8403.* Richly appointed hotel set in a classic Regency town house. Includes breakfast. 36 rooms.

Number Sixteen (B&B) ✪✪-✪✪✪ *16 Sumner Place, SW7 3EG; tel. 589 5232, fax 584 8615.* Attractively furnished Victorian town house with garden and conservatory. 36 rooms.

Regency ✪✪✪ *100–105 Queen's Gate, SW7 5AG; tel. 370 4595, fax 370 5555.* Elegant traditional hotel with well-appointed rooms, each with its own jacuzzi. 210 rooms.

VICTORIA (0171)

Chesham House Hotel ✪ *64–66 Ebury Street, SW1 W9QD; tel. 730 8513.* Reasonable basic accommodation in classic Georgian terraced house dating from 1825. 23 rooms.

Collin House ✪-✪✪ *104 Ebury Street, SW1W 9QD; tel. 730 8031, fax 730 8031.* Friendly hosts provide good basic accommodation in a Victorian town house. 13 rooms.

Ebury House Hotel ✪ *102 Ebury Street, SW1 W9QD; tel. 730 1350.* Friendly hosts offer small bright rooms in a 200-year-old building near Victoria station. 12 rooms.

Enrico (B&B) ✪ *77–79 Warwick Way SW1 V1QP; tel. 834 9538.* Cheap accommodation in pristine small rooms. 26 rooms.

Goring ✪✪✪-✪✪✪✪ *15 Beeston Place, Grosvenor Gardens, SW1W DJW; tel. 396-9000, fax 834 4393.* Family owned since 1910, with a claim to be London's best small hotel. Quiet location with garden. 79 rooms.

Grosvenor Thistle ✪✪✪ *101 Buckingham Palace Road, SW1W 03J; tel. 834 9494, fax 630 1978.* Grand old Victorian hotel with large, traditionally decorated rooms right beside the Victoria train station. 366 rooms.

Hamilton House (B&B) ✪ *60 Warwick Way, SW1V 1SA; tel. 821 7113, fax 630 0806.* Small hotel conveniently located for the West End. 37 rooms.

Melita (B&B) ✪ *35 Charlwood Street, SW1Y 2DU; tel. 828 0471, fax 932 0988.* Basic but homely accommodation in a 19th-century terraced house. 19 rooms.

Oxford House (B&B) ✪ *92–94 Cambridge Street, SW1V 4Q8; tel. 834 6467, fax 834 0225.* Friendly, comfortable accommodation in a 150-year-old terraced house. Quiet street. 17 rooms.

Romany House Hotel ✪ *35 Longmoore Street, SW1V 1JQ; tel. 834 5553.* This characterful house is reputed to date back to the 15th century, and provides bargain accommodation. 10 rooms.

Rubens ✪✪✪-✪✪✪✪ *Buckingham Palace Road, SW1W 0PS; tel. 834 6600, fax 828 5401.* Traditional-style hotel recently refurbished, opposite the Royal Mews, where the royal family's stately coaches are housed. Includes breakfast. 189 rooms.

Stakis St. Ermin's ✪✪ *2 Caxton Street, SW1H 0QW; tel. 222 7888, fax 222 6914.* Superb Edwardian building with opulent original features, set in a quiet street in the heart of Westminster. 290 rooms.

Windermere (B&B) ✪✪-✪✪ *142–44 Warwick Way, SW1V 4JE; tel. 834 5163, fax 630 8831.* Comfortable and attractively furnished accommodation in two charming early Victorian houses close to the station. Friendly service. 18 rooms.

Recommended Restaurants

Restaurants are listed alphabetically according to location. Prices quoted are per person and include starter, mid-priced main course and dessert, but not wine, coffee or service. A cheaper fixed-price menu is usually on offer at lunchtimes at the more expensive establishments.

✪	Lower-priced (under £20)
✪✪	Medium-priced £20–£30
✪✪✪	Expensive (above £30)

A two-part price band (eg. ✪–✪✪) indicates that there is a clear price distinction between lunch and dinner, or that the restaurant has two very different dining areas. Where a restaurant is unlicensed you may take along your own wine.

It is always a good idea to telephone in advance to check opening times of restaurants, as they vary considerably.

BLOOMSBURY (0171)
Museum Street Café
✪ *47 Museum Street, WC1; tel. 405 3211.* Award-winning Modern British cuisine served in basic surroundings. Highly popular. Unlicensed.

North Sea Fish Restaurant ✪ *7 Leigh Street, WC1; tel. 387 5892.* Upmarket fish and chip restaurant featuring sardines, salmon and sole as well as classic British fish and chips.

CHELSEA (0171)
Como Lario ✪ *22 Holbein Place, SW1; tel. 730 9046.* Old-style Italian food, good atmosphere with loyal regulars. Situated just off fashionable Sloane Square.

Ed's Easy Diner ✪ *362 King's Road, SW3; tel. 352 1956.* One of a chain of American-style diners serving burgers and fries, milkshakes, etc. Very popular.

Fulham Road ✪✪✪ *257–259 Fulham Road, SW3; tel. 351 7823.* Excellent innovative English cusine. Fresh fish dishes are a speciality.

The English Garden ✪✪✪ *10 Lincoln Street, SW3; tel. 584 7272.* Excellent modern and traditional British cusine. Ask for a table in the Victorian conservatory.

La Tante Claire ✪✪✪ *68 Royal Hospital Road, SW3; tel. 352 6045.* First-class French restaurant famous for its innovative cuisine. Beautiful setting.

THE CITY (0171)

Sweetings ✪ *39 Queen Victoria Street, EC4; tel. 248 3062.* Traditional 150-year-old fish restaurant. Tiny and immensely popular; you may have to queue.

CHINATOWN (0171)

Chuen Cheng Ku ✪✪ *17 Wardour Street, W1; tel. 437 1398.* This large, busy restaurant is one of the best places to try *dim sum* (served until 5:45 p.m.).

Fung Shing ✪✪ *15 Lisle Street, WC2; tel. 437-1539.* High quality food is served in this authentic Cantonese restaurant.

Mr Kong ✪✪ *21 Lisle Street, WC2; tel. 437 7341.* One of Chinatown's leading restaurants. Innovative dishes and old favourites; always popular.

Poon's ✪-✪✪ *27 Lisle Street, WC2; tel. 437 4549.* Scruffy and cramped, this is the original branch of Poons where the food is a Chinatown legend.

Wong Kei ✪ *41 Wardour Street, W1; tel. 437 6833.* Enormously popular Chinese restaurant. Always noisy and hectic; expect to share a table.

COVENT GARDEN (0171)

Bertorelli's ✪✪ *44a Floral Street, WC2; tel. 836 3969.* Very busy, fashionable restaurant serving pasta and salads.

Café Pelican ✪✪✪-✪✪✪ *45 St. Martin's Lane, WC2; tel. 379 0309.* Lively French brasserie serving drinks or full meals from 11 a.m. till 2 a.m. Terrace seating and jazz pianist every evening.

The Calabash ✪ *38 King's Street, WC2; tel. 836 1976.* In the basement of the Africa Centre, serving African dishes.

Food for Thought ✪ *31 Neal Street, WC2; tel. 836 0239.* A tiny basement restaurant serving vegetarian dishes. Immensely popular; excellent value.

Mon Plaisir ✪✪✪ *21 Monmouth Street, WC2; tel. 836 7243.* Traditional, friendly and informal French bistro/restaurant.

Orso ✪✪✪ *27 Wellington Street, WC2; tel. 240 5269.* Inspired Tuscan cooking in a lively atmosphere.

Porter's ✪✪ *17 Henrietta Street, WC2; tel. 836 6466.* Traditional British pies, apple crumble, and bread-and-butter pudding are the mainstays at this lively, good-value restaurant.

Rules ✪✪✪ *35 Maiden Lane, WC2; tel. 836 5314.* London's oldest restaurant serving traditional English fare. An historical landmark whose one-time clients include Dickens, Thackeray, and Edward VII.

Simpson's-in-the-Strand ✪✪✪ *100 Strand, WC2; tel. 836 9112.* Superlative traditional food in Ed-wardian surroundings. *The* place in London for roast beef and york-shire pudding. Jacket and tie.

EAST END (0171)

Bloom's ✪ *90 Whitechapel High Street, E1; tel. 247 6001/6835.* London's most acclaimed kosher restaurant.

Clifton ✪ *126 Brick Lane, E1; tel. 247 2364.* This is one of the many excellent value curry houses to be found in Brick Lane.

KENSINGTON (0171)

Cibo ✪✪ *3 Russell Gardens, W14; tel. 371 6271.* The best of modern Italian food in a small, fashionable place.

Leith's ✪✪✪ *92 Kensington Park Road, W11; tel. 229 4481.* A delightful restaurant set in an elegant Victorian terraced house. Modern European cuisine.

Phoenicia ✪-✪✪ *11 Abingdon Road, W8; tel. 937 0120.* Excellent Lebanese and Middle Eastern food. Go at lunch time for the all-you-can-eat buffet.

KNIGHTSBRIDGE (0171)

Khun Akorn ✪✪ *136 Brompton Road, SW3; tel. 225 2688.* Authentic Thai food in elegant and formal surroundings.

San Lorenzo ✪✪✪ *22 Beauchamp Place, SW3; tel. 584 1074.* Fashionable Italian restaurant.

MARYLEBONE & REGENT'S PARK (0171)

Woodlands ✪ *77 Marylebone Lane, W1; tel. 486 3862.* Excellent Southern Indian vegetarian cuisine.

MAYFAIR & PICCADILLY (0171)

Le Gavroche ✪✪✪ *43 Upper Brook Street, W1; tel. 408 0881.* London's only Michelin 3-star restaurant. World-class French *haute cuisine*. Jacket and tie.

Greig's Grill ✪✪-✪✪✪ *26 Bruton Place, W1; tel. 629 5613.* Devoted to steak, Greig's serves some of the best meat in town, and has a huge list of clarets.

Hard Rock Café ✪✪ *150 Old Park Lane, W1; tel. 629 0382 (no booking).* London's original burger joint; long queues, loud music, wonderful pop memorabilia.

Langan's Brasserie ✪✪ *55 Stratton Street, W1; tel. 493 6437.* Superb French cuisine in a fashionable restaurant co-owned by British film actor Michael Caine. Live music in the evening.

Suntory ✪✪✪ *72–73 St. James's Street, SW1; tel. 409 0201.* London's most opulent Japanese restaurant. Excellent menu.

Tiddy Dols ✪✪ *55 Shepherd Market, W1; tel. 499 2357.* A quintessentially English restaurant housed in an 18th-century building. Ginger bread pudding is their speciality.

Veeraswamy ✪✪ *99-101 Regent Street, W1; tel. 734 1401.*
The oldest and most upmarket of London's Indian restaurants, opened in 1927.

NORTH LONDON (0171)

Lemonia ✪ *89 Regent's Park Road, NW1; tel. 586 7454.*
Popular Greek-Cypriot restaurant with a lively atmosphere.

Odette's ✪✪ *130 Regent's Park Road, NW1; tel. 586 5486.*
Three-storey Mediterranean wine bar and restaurant with a menu that changes daily.

NOTTING HILL & PORTOBELLO (0171)

L'Artiste Assoiffé ✪ *122 Kensington Park Road, W11; tel.
727 4714.* Lively and relaxed French restaurant full of Portobello Market bric-a-brac and characters.

Clarke's ✪✪-✪✪✪ *124 Kensington Church St, W8; tel. 221
9225.* Highly acclaimed modern British cuisine. Set menu only on weekday evenings.

First Floor ✪✪ *186 Portobello Road, W11; tel. 243 0072.*
Modern, international cuisine in a trendy establishment on Portobello Road. Menu changes daily.

Geales ✪ *2–4 Farmer Street, W8; tel. 727 7969.* Cheap and cheerful fish restaurant. Terrifically popular, and for good reason.

Julie's ✪✪ *135 Portland Road, W11; tel. 229 8331.* Creative, modern European cuisine in a chic restaurant with a lovely covered courtyard.

Khan's ✪ *13–15 Westbourne Grove, W2; tel. 727 5420.* An Indian institution for Londoners on a budget. Atmospheric and bustling, though service can be abrupt.

SOHO (0171)

Au Jardin des Gourmets ✪-✪✪ *5 Greek Street, W1; tel. 437
1816.* Long-established Soho favourite serving superb modern French cuisine. The wine list is formidable, and includes some old and rare clarets.

Bahn Thai ✪✪–✪✪✪ *21a Frith Street, W1; tel. 437 8504.* Small, dark restaurant, one of London's best Thai eating places. The menu includes a number of vegetarian dishes.

Bistro Bruno ✪✪ *63 Frith Street, W1; tel. 734 4545.* Excellent, imaginative restaurant with a French flavour. Charming Gallic atmosphere.

Gay Hussar ✪-✪✪ *2 Greek Street, W1; tel. 437 0973.* Fine old-fashioned establishment serving hearty Hungarian (and Transylvanian) fare. A haunt of politicians and literary folk.

Kaya ✪✪ *22–25 Dean Street, W1; tel. 437 6630.* A calm atmosphere in which to sample Korean delights. The helpful manageress will explain the menu.

Lindsay House ✪-✪✪ *21 Romilly Street, W1; tel. 439 0450.* Superb Modern British cooking in a delightful 17th-century establishment. Outstanding value set lunch; extensive wine list.

Melati ✪ *21 Great Windmill Street, W1; tel. 734 6964.* An immensely popular Indonesian/Malaysian restaurant with an excellent reputation.

Saigon ✪✪ *15 Frith Street, W1; tel. 437 7109.* Fashionable Vietnamese restaurant serving Soho trendies. The set menu is good value.

SOUTH KENSINGTON (0171)

Bibendum ✪✪✪ *81 Fulham Road, SW3; tel. 581 5817.* Set in the beautiful Art Nouveau Michelin Building, Bibendum's reputation stretches far and wide. Restaurant upstairs; oyster bar downstairs. Book for dinner at least a fortnight in advance.

Bombay Brasserie ✪✪ *Courtfield Road, SW7; tel. 370 4040.* Possibly London's best and most atmospheric Indian restaurant. Eat-all-you-like lunch buffet is very good value.

ABOUT BERLITZ

In 1878 Professor Maximilian Berlitz had a revolutionary idea about making language learning accessible and enjoyable. One hundred and twenty years later these same principles are still successfully at work.

For language instruction, translation and interpretation services, cross-cultural training, study abroad programs, and an array of publishing products and additional services, visit any one of our more than 350 Berlitz Centers in over 40 countries.

Please consult your local telephone directory for the Berlitz Center nearest you or visit our web site at http://www.berlitz.com.

Helping the World Communicate

Other Berlitz titles include:

Africa
Kenya
Morocco
South Africa
Tunisia

Asia, Middle East
Bali and Lombok
China
Egypt
Hong Kong
India
Indonesia
Israel
Japan
Malaysia
Singapore
Sri Lanka
Thailand

Australasia
Australia
New Zealand
Sydney

Austria, Switzerland
Austrian Tyrol
Switzerland
Vienna

Belgium, The Netherlands
Amsterdam
Bruges and Ghent
Brussels

British Isles
Channel Islands
Dublin
Edinburgh
Ireland
London
Scotland

Caribbean, Latin America
Bahamas
Bermuda
Cancún and Cozumel
Cuba
French West Indies
Jamaica
Mexico
Puerto Rico
Southern Caribbean
Virgin Islands

Central and Eastern Europe
Budapest
Czech Republic
Moscow and St Petersburg
Prague

France
Brittany
Côte d'Azur
Dordogne
Euro Disney Resort
France
Normandy
Paris
Provence

Germany
Berlin
Munich

Greece, Cyprus and Turkey
Athens
Corfu
Crete
Cyprus
Greek Islands
Istanbul
Rhodes
Turkey

Italy and Malta
Florence
Italy
Malta
Milan and the Lakes
Naples
Rome
Sicily
Venice

North America
Boston
California
Canada
Disneyland and the Theme Parks of Southern California
Florida
Hawaii
Los Angeles
New Orleans
New York
San Francisco
USA
Walt Disney World and Orlando
Washington D.C.

Portugal
Algarve
Lisbon
Madeira
Portugal

Scandinavia
Copenhagen
Helsinki
Oslo and Bergen
Stockholm
Sweden

Spain
Barcelona
Canary Islands
Costa Blanca
Costa del Sol
Costa Dorada and Tarragona
Ibiza and Formentera
Madrid
Mallorca and Menorca
Spain

Special
Channel Hopper's Wine Guide (UK only)

Also from Berlitz

- **Today language series**
- **Basic language series**
- **Cassette Packs**
- **Phrase Books**
- **Bilingual Dictionaries**
- **Essential series**
- **Grammar, Verb, and Vocabulary Handbooks**
- **Basic and Intermediate Workbooks**
- **Berlitz Kids™ series**
- **Pocket Guides to more than 100 destinations**

Berlitz®

London
pocket guide

The acclaimed Berlitz *Pocket Guides* are packed with a world of information Each guide is carefully researched, fun to read, and easy to use.

Whether planning a trip to London for business or pleasure, this guide will help you get the most from your trip.

- Information about must-see sights, transportation, and emergencies
- Detailed maps and stunning photography
- Latest recommendations for hotels, restaurants, shopping, sports, festivals, and nightlife

ISBN 2-8315-63

9 782831 563268

US $ 8.95 £ 4.95

T2-AZW-300